D0056819

OLD-TIME PUNISHMENTS.

BANK RESTRICTION NOTE

Specimen of a Bank Note — not to be imitated.

Submitted to the Consideration of the Bank-Directors and the inspection of the Public.

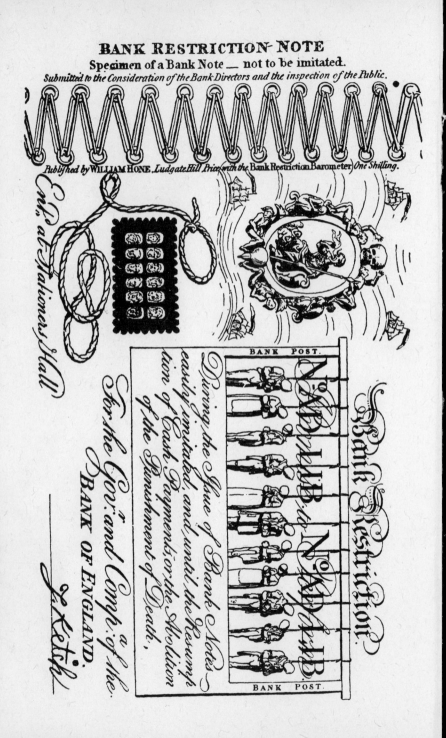

Published by WILLIAM HONE, Ludgate Hill. Price (with the Bank Restriction Barometer) One Shilling.

Old-Time

PUNISHMENTS.

BY

WILLIAM ANDREWS, F.R.H.S.,

DORSET PRESS
New York

This edition published by Dorset Press,
a division of Marboro Books Corporation.
1991 Dorset Press

ISBN 0-88029-703-4

Printed in the United States of America
M 9 8 7 6 5 4

To

ALDERMAN JOHN LOVE SEATON, J.P.,

THE PARK, HULL,

This Volume

IS

RESPECTFULLY INSCRIBED.

W. A.

Contents.

Preface.

IN the year 1881, I produced a small work, entitled, "Punishments in the Olden Time," and, to my surprise, in less than three months four thousand copies were sold. After that number had been published, and numerous flattering notices given by the critical press, I resolved to write a larger book on the same subject. The result of my labours is presented in the following pages. I hope this volume contains interesting information which does not usually come under the notice of the reader, but nevertheless important in throwing light on the history of bygone times.

In the preparation of this book, I have consulted several hundred works, and drawn facts from ancient records which still remain in manuscript; and the daily and weekly newspapers have also supplied me with items I have deemed worthy of quotation. It will be found that where I have obtained information due acknowledgment is given.

My gratitude is due to the following, who have cheerfully and freely given me valuable assistance: Mrs. G. Linnæus Banks; Mr. W. E. A. Axon; Dr. T. N. Brushfield; Mr. Alfred Burton; Mr. E. H. Coleman; the Rev. J. Charles Cox, LL.D.; Mr. Walter Hamilton; Mr. Jno. Nicholson; Mr. T. Tindall Wildridge; the late Llewellynn Jewitt, F.S.A.; and the late Rev. Charles Rogers, LL.D.

In conclusion, I have only to repeat some words I have previously used, namely: that if this volume meets with a similar welcome from the press and the public to that which has been awarded to my former works, I shall have every reason to feel thankful.

WILLIAM ANDREWS.

HULL LITERARY CLUB,
    December 1st, 1890.

OLD-TIME PUNISHMENTS.

The Ducking=Stool.

SCOLDING women in the olden times were treated as offenders against the public peace, and for their transgressions were subjected to several cruel modes of punishment. The Corporations of towns during the Middle Ages made their own regulations for punishing persons guilty of crimes which were not rendered penal by the laws of the land. The punishments for correcting scolds differed greatly in various parts of the country. It is clear, from a careful study of the history of mediæval times, that virtue and amiability amongst the middle and lower classes, generally speaking, did not prevail. The free use of the tongue gave rise to riots and feuds to such an extent that it is difficult for us to realise at the present day. A strong feeling against scolding women came down to a late period. Readers of

Boswell's delightful "Life of Johnson" will remember how the burly, but dear old Doctor, in reply to a remark made by a celebrated Quaker lady, Mrs. Knowles, observed : "Madam, we have different modes of restraining evil—stocks for men, a ducking-stool for women, and a pound for beasts."

The cucking-stool in the early history of England must not be confounded with the ducking-stool. They were two distinct machines. It appears, from a record in the "Domesday Book," that as far back as the days of Edward the Confessor, any man or woman detected giving false measure in the city of Chester was fined four shillings ; and for brewing bad ale, was placed in the *cathedra stercoris.* It was a degrading mode of chastisement, the culprits being seated in the chair at their own doors or in some public place. At Leicester, in 1467, the local authorities directed "scolds to be punished by the Mayor on a cuck-stool before their own doors, and then carried to the four gates of the town." According to Borlase's "Natural History of Cornwall," in that part of the country the cucking-stool was used "as a seat of infamy, where strumpets and scolds, with bare feet and head, were condemned to abide the derision of those that passed by, for such as the bailiffs of the manors, which had the privilege of such jurisdiction, did approve." Ale-wives in Scotland in bygone times who sold bad ale were placed in the cucking-stool. In the year 1555, we learn from Thomas Wright that " it was enacted by the queen-regent of Scotland that itinerant singing women should be put on the cuck-stoles of every burgh or town; and the first 'Homily against Contention,' part 3, published in 1562, sets forth that 'in all well-ordered cities common brawlers and scolders be punished with a notable kind of paine, as to be *set on* the cucking-stole, pillory, or such like.' By the statute of 3 Henry VIII., carders and spinners of wool who were convicted of fraudulent practices were to be *sett upon* the pillorie or the cukkyng-stole, man or woman, as the case shall require." We agree with Mr. Wright when he observes that the preceding passages are worded in such a manner as not to lead us to suppose that the offenders were ducked. In the course of time the terms cucking and ducking stools became synonymous, and implied the machines for the ducking of scolds in water.

An intelligent Frenchman, named Misson, visited England about 1700, and has left on record one of the best descriptions of a ducking-stool that has been written. It occurs in a work entitled "Travels in England." "The way of punishing scolding women," he writes, "is pleasant enough. They fasten an arm chair to the end of two beams, twelve or fifteen feet long, and parallel to each other, so that these two pieces of wood, with their two ends, embrace the chair, which hangs between them upon a sort of axle, by which means it plays freely, and always remains in the natural horizontal position in which the chair should be, that a person may sit conveniently in it, whether you raise it or let it down. They set up a post on the bank of a pond or river, and over this post they lay, almost in equilibrio, the two pieces of wood, at one end of which the chair hangs just over the water. They place the woman in this chair, and so plunge her into the water, as often as the sentence directs, in order to cool her immoderate heat." In some instances the ducking was carried to such an extent as to cause death. An old chap-book, without date, is entitled, " Strange and Wonderful Relation of the Old Woman who was Drowned

at Ratcliff Highway a fortnight ago." It appears
from this work that the poor woman was dipped
too often, for at the conclusion of the operation
she was found to be dead. We reproduce from
this quaint chap-book a picture of the ducking-
stool. It will be observed that it is not a
stationary machine, but one which can be wheeled

DUCKING-STOOL FROM A CHAP-BOOK.

to and from the water. Similar ducking-stools
were usually kept in some convenient building,
and ready to be brought out for immediate use,
but in many places the ducking-stools were permanent fixtures.

Many of the older poets and dramatists refer
to this ancient mode of punishment. Lord
Dorset thus alludes to it :

"She in the ducking-stool should take her seat,
Dressed like herself in a great chair of state."

Say Beaumont and Fletcher in the "Tamer Tamed:"

> " We'll ship them out in cuck-stoles;
>   There they'll sail
> As brave as Columbus did."

In the year 1665 was issued " Homer a la Mode," and respecting a woman says the author:

> " She belonged to Billingsgate,
>   And often times had rid in state,
>   And sate i' the bottome of a poole,
>   Inthroned in a cucking-stool."

Butler in his " Hudibras " has an allusion to this subject.   He says:

> " These mounted on a chair curule,
>   Which moderns call a cucking-stoole,
>   March proudly to the river side,
>   And o'er the waves in triumph ride.
>   Like Dukes of Venice who are said
>   The Adriatic Sea to wed,
>   And have a gentler wife than those
>   For whom the State decrees these shows."

Nash, in his notes to " Hudibras," adverts to having seen " a stool of this kind near the bridge at Evesham, in Worcestershire, not above eight miles from Strensham, the place of the poet's birth."   The erudite historian of Leominster, the Rev. George Fyler Townsend, M.A., says that in Butler's lines it is evident that he referred to a

moveable machine, and as the poet lived in the
Castle of Ludlow, within a few miles of Loe-
minster, it is very probable that he had the
ducking-stool of the town in his memory when he
wrote his poem. Vincent Bourne died in 1747,
and a few years previously published a volume of
verse in Latin and English, and in one of his
poems writes as follows :

> " Near many a stream was wont to meet us
> A stool, to broils a sure quietus.
> It curb'd the tongue, the passions rein'd,
> And reason's empire firm maintained.
> Astride it set but a Xanthippe,
> Then twice or thrice virago dip ye ;
> And not a lambkin on the lea
> Will leave the stream more meek than she.
> A Lethe o'er her memory shed,
> The very shades of anger fled.
> Cool grows the fever of the breast,
> And surging passions seek to rest.
> The lesson ex cathedrâ taught
> Here balance in the scale of thought ;
> Then say if e'er Socratic school
> Such lesson taught as ducking-stool."

Vincent Bourne, the author of the foregoing
spirited lines, was one of the under-masters at
Westminster School. It will be noticed that he
spoke of the custom as a thing of the past, but it
remained a public institution for many years after
the poet had passed away. Gay, another poet of

the eighteenth century, in his pastoral of "The
Duress" makes his heroine say :

> "I'll speed me to the pool where the high stool,
> On the long plank, hangs o'er the muddy pool :
> That stool, the dread of every scolding quean—
> Yet sure a lover should not die so mean."

Old municipal accounts and records contain many
references to this subject.   Cole, a Cambridge
antiquary, collected numerous curious items connected with this theme.   In some extracts made
from the proceedings of the Vice-Chancellor's
Court, in the reign of Elizabeth, it is stated :
"Jane Johnson, adjudged to the ducking-stool
for scolding, and commuted her penance." The
next person does not appear to have been so for-
tunate as Jane Johnson, who avoided punishment
by paying a fine of about five shillings. It is
recorded : "Katherine Saunders, accused by the
churchwardens of Saint Andrews for a common
scold and slanderer of her neighbours, was
adjudged to the ducking-stool."

We find in one of Cole's manuscript volumes,
preserved in the British Museum, a graphic
sketch of this ancient mode of punishment. He
says : "In my time, when I was a boy, I lived
with my grandmother in the great corner house

at the foot, 'neath the Magdalen College, Cambridge, and rebuilt since by my uncle, Joseph Cook. I remember to have seen a woman ducked for scolding. The chair was hung by a pulley fastened to a beam about the middle of the bridge, in which [he means the chair, of course, not the bridge] the woman was confined, and let down three times, and then taken out. The bridge was then of timber, before the present stone bridge of one arch was built. The ducking-stool was constantly hanging in its place, and on the back of it were engraved devils laying hold of scolds, etc. Some time afterwards a new chair was erected in the place of the old one, having the same devices carved upon it, and well painted and ornamented. When the new bridge of stone was erected, in 1754, this chair was taken away, and I lately saw the carved and gilt back of it nailed up by the shop of one Mr. Jackson, a whitesmith, in the Butcher's Row, behind the Town Hall, who offered it to me, but I did not know what to do with it. In October, 1776, I saw in the old Town Hall a third ducking-stool, of plain oak, with an iron bar in front of it, to confine the person in the seat, but I made no inquiries about it. I mention these things as the

practice of ducking scolds in the river seems now
to be totally laid aside." Mr. Cole died in 1782,
so did not long survive the writing of the foregoing curious notes.

The Sandwich ducking-stool was embellished
with men and women scolding. On the cross-bar
were carved the following words :

"Of members ye tonge is worst or best,—an
Yll tonge oft doeth breede unrest."

Boys, in his "Collections for the History of
Sandwich," published in 1792, remarks that the

ducking - stool was
preserved in the
second storey of the
Town Hall, along
with other arms,
offensive and defen-
sive, of the Trained
Bands. Boys's book
includes some im-
portant information
on old-time punish-
ments. In the year

SANDWICH DUCKING-STOOL.

1534, it is recorded that two women were
banished from Sandwich for immorality. To
deter them from coming back to the town it was

decided that "if they return, one of them is to suffer the pain of sitting over the coqueen-stool, and the other is to be set three days in the stocks, with an allowance of only bread and water, and afterwards to be placed in the coqueen-stool and dipped to the chin." A woman, in the year 1568, was "carted and banished." At Sandwich, Ipswich, and some other places, as a punishment for scolding and other offences it was not an uncommon thing to compel the transgressors to carry a wooden mortar round the town.

Respecting the cost of erecting a ducking-stool, we find a curious and detailed account in the parish books of Southam, Warwickshire, for the year of grace 1718. In the first place, a man was sent from Southam to Daventry to make a drawing of the ducking-stool of that town, at a cost of three shillings and twopence. In the next place, the sum of one pound one shilling and eightpence is charged for labour and material in making and fixing the engine of punishment. An entry of ten shillings is made for painting it, which appears a rather heavy amount when we observe that the carpenter only charged a little over a pound for labour and timber. Perhaps, like the good folks of Sandwich, the authorities of

Southam had their chair ornamented with artistic
portraits and enriched with poetic quotations.
The blacksmith had to furnish ironwork, etc., at
a cost of four shillings and sixpence. For carrying the stool to its proper place half-a-crown was
paid. Lastly, nine shillings and sixpence had to
be expended to make the pond deeper, so that
the ducking-stool might work in a satisfactory
manner. The total amount reaches £2 11s. 4d.
At Coventry, in the same county, we find traces
of two ducking-stools, and respecting them Mr.
W. G. Fretton, F.S.A., supplies us with some
curious details. The following notes are drawn
from the Leet Book, under date of October 11th,
1597 : "Whereas there are divers and sundrie
disordered persons (women) within this citie that
be scolds, brawlers, disturbers, and disquieters
of theire neighbors, to the great offence of
Almightie God and the breach of Her Majestie's
peace : for the reformation of such abuses, it is
ordered and enacted at this leet, that if any disordered and disquiet persons of this citie do from
henceforth scold or brawle with their neighbo'rs
or others, upon complaint thereof to the Alderman of the ward made, or to the Maior for the
time being, they shall be committed to the cooke-

stoole lately appointed for the punishment of such offenders, and thereupon be punished for their deserts, except they, or everie of them, do presentlie paie iijs iijd for their redemption from that punishment to the use of the poore of this citie."

The old accounts of the City of Coventry contain numerous items bearing on the ducking-stool.

In a volume of " Miscellaneous Poems," by Benjamin West, of Weedon Beck, Northampton-shire, published in 1780, we find some lines entitled, " The Ducking-Stool," as follows :

"There stands, my friend, in yonder pool,
An engine called the ducking-stool,
By legal pow'r commanded down,
The joy and terror of the town,
If jarring females kindle strife,
Give language foul or lug the coif ;
If noisy dames should once begin
To drive the house with horrid din,
Away, you cry, you'll grace the stool,
We'll teach you how your tongue to rule.
The fair offender fills the seat,
In sullen pomp, profoundly great,
Down in the deep the stool descends,
But here, at first, we miss our ends ;
She mounts again, and rages more
Than ever vixen did before.
So, throwing water on the fire
Will make it but burn up the higher ;

If so, my friend, pray let her take
A second turn into the lake,
And, rather than your patience lose,
Thrice and again repeat the dose.
No brawling wives, no furious wenches,
No fire so hot, but water quenches.
In Prior's skilful lines we see
For these another recipe:
A certain lady, we are told
(A lady, too, and yet a scold),
Was very much reliev'd, you'll say
By water, yet a different way;
A mouthful of the same she'd take,
Sure not to scold, if not to speak."

A footnote to the poem states: "To the honour of the fair sex in the neighbourhood of R——y, this machine has been taken down (as useless) several years." Most probably, says Mr. Jewitt, the foregoing refers to Rugby. In the old accounts of that town several items occur, as for example:

1721. June 5. Paid for a lock for ye ducking-
            stool, and spent in towne business ...   ...   1s.   2d.
1739. Sept. 25. Ducking-stool repaired. And
            Dec. 21, 1741. A chain for ducking-stool ...   2s.   4d.

Mr. Pretty, F.S.A., in a note to Mr. Llewellynn Jewitt, which is inserted in *The Reliquary* for January, 1861, states that the Rugby ducking-stool "was placed on the west side of the horse-pool, near the footpath leading from the Clifton

Road towards the new churchyard. Part of the
posts to which it was affixed were visible until
very lately, and the National School is now
erected on its site. The last person who underwent the punishment was a man, for beating his
wife, about forty years since; but although the
ducking-stool has been long removed, the ceremony of immersion in the horsepond was recently
inflicted on an inhabitant for brutality towards
his wife." The Rugby ducking-stool was of the
trebuchet form, somewhat similar to one which
was in use at Broadwater, near Worthing, and
which has been frequently engraved. We reproduce an illustration of the latter from the *Wiltshire Archæological Magazine*, which represents it

DUCKING-STOOL, BROADWATER, NEAR WORTHING.

as it appeared in the year 1776. It was in existence at a much later period. Its construction was

very simple, consisting of a short post let into the ground at the edge of a pond, bearing on the top a transverse beam, one end of which carried the stool, while the other end was secured by a rude chair. We are told, in an old description of this ducking-stool, that the beam could be moved horizontally, so as to bring the seat to the edge of the pond, and that when the beam was moved back, so as to place the seat and the person in it over the pond, the beam was worked up and down like a see-saw, and so the person in the seat was ducked. When the machine was not in use, the end of the beam which came on land was secured to a stump in the ground by a padlock, to prevent the village children from ducking each other.

Mr. T. Tindall Wildridge, author of several important local historical works, and Keeper of the Records of Kingston-upon-Hull, informs us that the great profligacy of that port frequently gave rise in olden times to very stringent exercise of the magisterial authority. Not infrequently this was at the direct instigation and sometimes command of the Archbishop of York. Occasionally the cognisance of offences was retrospective. Thus, in November, 1620, it was resolved by the

Bench of Magistrates, then composed of the Aldermen of the town, that such as had been "faltie for bastardes" should be carted about the town and afterwards "ducked in the water for their faults, for which they have hitherto escaped punishment." At a little later period, in England, in the days of the Commonwealth, it was enacted on May 14th, 1650, that adultery should be punished with death, but there is not any record of the law taking effect. The Act was repealed at the Restoration. About a century before this period, namely, in 1563, in the Scottish Parliament this crime was made a capital offence. In New England, in the year 1662, several men and women suffered for this crime. Our Saxon ancestors were extremely severe in respect to adultery. In the earlier Saxon era it was the custom to burn the adulteress, and over her ashes to erect a gibbet, on which the adulterer was hanged. Coming down to the reign of Canute (1016), we find that he "adjudged the man to exile, and the woman to have her nose and ears cut off." Resuming our notes on the Hull ducking-stool, we find, according to Hadley, the historian, that in the year 1731 Mr. Beilby, who held the office of town's husband, was ordered to

take care that a ducking-stool should be provided
at the Southend for the benefit of scolds and
unquiet women. Six years later, John Hilbert
published a view of the town of Hull, in which is
a representation of the ducking-stool. Mr. M. C.
Peck exhibited this very rare engraving at a
meeting of the Hull Literary Club, and it is supposed to be the only picture in which a drawing
of the Hull ducking-stool is given. Mr. Wildridge
has found traces of another local ducking-stool.
He states that in some accounts belonging to the
eighteenth century is a charge for tarring a ducking-stool situated on the Haven-side, on the
East-side of the town.

At the neighbouring town of Beverley are
traces of this old mode of punishment, and in the
town records are several notes bearing on the
subject. Brewers of bad beer and bakers of bad
bread as well as scolding women were placed in
the ducking-stool.

The Leeds ducking-stool was at Quarry Hill,
near the Spa. At the Court of Quarter Sessions,
held in the town in July, 1694, it was "ordered
that Anne, the wife of Phillip Saul, a person
of lewd behaviour, be ducked for daily making
strife and discord amongst her neighbours." A

similar order was made against Jane Milner and Elizabeth Wooler.

We find in the Session records of Wakefield, for 1602, the following : " Punishm⁺ of Hall and Robinson, scolds fforasmuch as Katherine Hall and M'garet Robinson, of Wakefield are great disturbers and disquieters of their neighbours w'thin the toune of Wakefield, by reason of their daily scolding and chydering, the one w'th the other, for reformacon whereof ytt it is ordered that if they doe hereafter continue their former course of life in scolding and brawling, that then John Mawde, the high constable there, shall cause them to be soundlye ducked or cucked on the cuckstool at Wakefield for said misdemeanour."

In the records of Wakefield Sessions, under date of October 5th, 1671, the following appears : " Forasmuch as Jane, the wife of William Farrett of Selby, shoemaker, stands indicted at this sessions for a common scold, to the great annoyance and disturbance of her neighbours, and breach of His Majesty's peace.   It is therefore ordered that the said Jane Farrett, for the said offence be openly ducked, and ducked three times over the head and ears by the constables of Selby aforesaid, for which this shall be their warrant."

At Bradford the ducking-stool was formerly at
the Beck, near to the Parish Church, and on the
formation of the canal it was removed, but only a
short distance from its original position.   Still
lingering in the West Riding of Yorkshire, we
find in the parish accounts of East Ardsley, the
following item :

1683-4.   Paid John Crookes for repairing stool ... 1s.   8d.

Norrisson Scatcherd, in his " History of Morley,"
and William Smith, in his " Morley Ancient and
Modern," give interesting details of the ducking-
stool at Morley.   Not far distant from Morley is
Calverley, and in the Constable's account of the
village it is stated :

1728.   Paid Jeremy Booth for powl for ducking-stool ... 2s.

At Haworth we have traces of this ancient mode
of punishment.   Says Mr. J. Horsfall Turner, at
Ilkley in bygone times, scolds were ducked in the
Wharfe, if unable to pay a fine of 6s. 8d.

Mr. Joseph Wilkinson, in his volume on Worsborough, near Barnsley, has some important
information on this theme.   " The ducking-stool,"
says Mr. Wilkinson, " was not only used as a
punishment for scolds and brawlers, but also for

brewers and bakers, who either in the one case sold ale in short measure or of bad quality, or, in the other, made bad bread or sold short weight. There is said to have been two ducking-ponds in the township—one in the village of Worsborough and another near to the Birdwell tollbar; and, judging from the frequency of their being repaired by the township, it would seem they were often brought into requisiton." The following extracts are drawn from the parish accounts:

1703.	For mending ye cuck-stool	£0	0	6
1721.	Ducking-stool mending	0	1	8
1725.	For mending and hanging ye cuck-stool ...	0	1	0
1730.	Pd. Thos. Moorhouse for mending ye stocks and cuck-stool	0	1	0
„	Pd. Jno. South for 2 staples for ye cucking-stool	0	0 ·	4
1731.	Thos. Moorhouse for mending ye ducking-stool	0	1	0
1734-5.	To ye ducking-stool mending	0	0	6
1736.	For mending ye ducking-stool	0	10	0
1737.	John Ellot, for ye ducking-stool and sheep-fold door	0	14	6

Mr. W. H. Dawson, the historian of Skipton, has devoted considerable attention to the old-time punishments of the town, and the first reference he was able to discover amongst the old accounts of the township is the following:

1734. October 2nd. To Wm. Bell, for ducking-stool making and wood	8s.	6d.

"This must," says Mr. Dawson, "surely mean that the chair was changed, for the amount is too small for the entire apparatus. In this case a ducking-stool must have existed before 1734, which is very likely." In the same Skipton township account-book is an entry as follows:

1743.   October.   Ben Smith for ducking-stool...   4s.   6d.

Twenty-five years later we find a payment as follows:

1768.   October 17th.   Paid John Brown
        for new ducking-stool   ...   ...   £1   0s.   11½d.

Mr. Dawson has not been able to discover the exact date when the ducking-stool fell into dis-use, but has good reason for believing that it was about 1770. We gather from a note sent to us by Mr. Dawson that: "A ducking-pond existed at Kirkby, although it had not been used within the memory of any living person. Scolds of both sexes were punished by being ducked; indeed, in the last observance of the custom, a tailor and his wife were ducked together, in view of a large gathering of people. The husband had applied for his wife to undergo the punishment on account of her quarrelsome nature, but the magistrate decided that one was not better than the

other, and he ordered a joint punishment! Back
to back, therefore, husband and wife were chaired
and dipped into the cold water of the pond!
Whether it was in remembrance of this old observance or not cannot be definitely said, but it
is, nevertheless, a fact that in East Lancashire, in
1880, a man who had committed some violation of
morals was forcibly taken by a mob, and dragged
several times through a pond until he had expressed penitence for his act."

We have found several allusions to the Derby
ducking-stool. Wooley, writing in 1772, states
that "over against the steeple [All Saint's] is St.
Mary's Gate, which leads down to the brook
near the west side of St. Werburgh's Church,
over which there is a bridge to Mr. Osborne's
mill, over the pool of which stands the ducking-
stool." Mr. Jewitt found particulars of a charge
made in 1729 for repairing it by a joiner named
Thomas Timmins:

To ye Cuckstool, the stoop	...	...	...	0 01 0
2 Foot and ½ of Ioyce for a Rayle	...	...	0 00 5
Ja. Ford, junr., ½ day at Cuckstool	...	...	0 00 7

The Chesterfield ducking-stool was pulled down
towards the close of the last century. It is
stated by Mr. Jewitt that in the latter part of

its existence it was chiefly used for punishing refractory paupers.

SCARBOROUGH DUCKING-STOOL.

The Scarborough ducking-stool was formerly placed on the old pier, and was last used about

the year 1795, when a Mrs. Gamble was ducked.
The chair is preserved in the Museum of the
Scarborough Philosophical Society. We are indebted to Dr. T. N. Brushfield for an excellent
drawing of it.

An object which attracts much attention from
visitors to the interesting museum at Ipswich
is the ducking-stool of
the town. We give
a carefully executed
drawing of it. It is
described as a strong-
backed arm-chair, with
a wrought-iron rod,
about an inch in dia-
meter, fastened to each
arm in front, meeting
in a segment of a circle
above; there is also

IPSWICH DUCKING-STOOL.

another iron rod affixed to the back, which
curves over the head of the person seated in the
chair, and is connected with the other at the top,
to the centre of which is fastened an iron ring
for the purpose of slinging the machine into the
river. It is plain and substantial, and has more
the appearance of solidity than antiquity in its

construction. We are told by the local historian
that in the Chamberlain's books are various entries for money paid to porters for taking down
the ducking-stool and assisting in the operation
of cooling, by its means, the inflammable passions
of some of the female inhabitants of Ipswich.

We give a spirited sketch of the Ipswich
ducking-stool, from the pencil of Campion, a local
artist. It is worthy of the pencil of Hogarth,
Gilray, or Cruikshank; indeed, it is often said
to be the production of the last-named artist,
but though after his style it is not his work.

There are traces in the Court-Book of St.
George's Gild of the use of the ducking-stool at
Norwich. Amongst other entries is one to the
effect that in 1597 a scold was ducked three times.

The ducking-stool at Nottingham, in addition
to being employed for correcting scolds, was used
for the exposure of females of bad repute. " It
consisted," says Mr. J. Potter Briscoe, F.R.H.S.,
" of a hollow box, which was sufficiently large to
admit of two persons being exposed at the same
time. Through holes in the side the heads of
the culprits were placed. In fact, the Nottingham cuck-stool was similar to a pillory. The last
time this ancient instrument of punishment was

brought into requisition was in 1731, when the
Mayor (Thomas Trigge) caused a female to be
placed in it for immorality, and left her to the
mercy of the mob, which ducked her so severely

IPSWICH DUCKING-STOOL.

that her death ensued shortly afterwards. The
Mayor, in consequence, was prosecuted, and the
Nottingham cuck-stool was ordered to be des-

troyed." In the Nottinghamshire records are traces of the ducking-stool at Southwell and Retford. The example at the latter town is traced back to an unusually early period.

The old ducking-stool of King's Lynn, Norfolk, may now be seen in the Museum of that town.

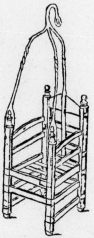

The annals of the borough contain numerous allusions to the punishment of women. In the year 1587, it is stated that for immoral conduct, John Wanker's wife and widow Parker were both carted. It is recorded that, in 1754, "one Elizabeth Neivel stood in the pillory, and that one Hannah Clark was ducked for scolding." There is mention of a woman named

DUCKING-STOOL, KING'S LYNN.

Howard standing in the pillory in 1782, but no particulars are given of her crime. In another chapter we advert to the boiling and burning to death of women at this town.

In a note written for us in 1881, by Mr. R. N. Worth, the historian of Plymouth, we are told that in Devon and Cornwall the ducking-stool was the usual means employed for inflicting punishment on scolding women. At Plymouth, the ducking-stool was erected at the Barbican, a site full of historic interest. From here Sir Walter Raleigh was conducted to his long imprisonment, followed by death on the scaffold. It was here that the Pilgrim Fathers bade adieu to the shores

of their native land to es-
tablish a New England
across the Atlantic. As
might be expected, the old
municipal accounts of Plymouth contain many curi-
ous and interesting items
bearing on the punish-
ment of women. Mr. W.
H. K. Wright, editor of
the "Western Antiquary,"
tells us, as recently as the
year 1808 the last person
was ducked. At Ply-
mouth, at the present
time, are preserved two

PLYMOUTH DUCKING-STOOL.

ducking-chairs, one in the Athenæum and the other in the office of the Borough Surveyor. Mr. Wright has kindly supplied illustrations of both. It will be observed that the chairs are made of iron.

The last time the Bristol ducking-stool was used was, it is said, in the year 1718. The Mayor gave instructions for the ducking of scolds, and the immersions took place at the weir.

We have numerous accounts of this engine of punishment in Lancashire. In the "Manchester Historical Recorder" we find it stated, in the year 1775 : "Manchester ducking-stool in use.

PLYMOUTH DUCKING-STOOL.

It was an open-bottomed chair of wood, placed upon a long pole balanced on a pivot, and suspended over the collection of water called the Pool House and Pool Fold. It was afterwards suspended over the Daubholes (Infirmary pond) and was used for the purpose of punishing scolds and prostitutes." We find, on examination of an old print, that it was similar to the example at Broadwater, of which we give a sketch. According to Mr. Richard Brooke's "Liverpool from 1775 to 1800," the ducking-stool was in use in 1779, by the authority of the magistrates. We have particulars of the ducking-stool at Preston, Kirkham, Burnley and other Lancashire towns.

At Wootton Bassett there was a tumbrel, which, until within the last few years, was perfect. The chair is still preserved by the Corporation of that town. We give a drawing of it from the *Wiltshire Archæological and Natural History Magazine.* We are told the machine, when complete, consisted of a chair, a pair of wheels, two

TUMBREL AT WOOTTON BASSETT.

long poles forming shafts, and a rope attached to each shaft, at about a foot from the end. The person to be ducked was tied in the chair, and the machine pushed into a pond called the Weir-pond, and the shafts being let go, the scold was lifted backwards into the water, the shafts flying up, and being recovered again by means of the ropes attached to them. The chair is of oak, and bears the date of 1686 on the back. In some places, millers, if detected stealing corn, were placed in the tumbrel.

The wheels of a tumbrel are preserved in the old church of St. Mary's, Warwick, and the chair, it is said, is still in the possession of an inhabitant of the town.

At Kingston-upon-Thames ducking was not infrequent. The Chamberlain's accounts include many items relating to the subject. We are disposed to believe, from the mention of three wheels, in a payment made in 1572, that here the engine of punishment was a tumbrel. The following amounts were paid in 1572 :

The making of the cucking-stool	8s.	0d.
Iron work for the same ..;	3s.	0d.
Timber for the same	7s.	6d.
Three brasses for the same, and three wheels ...	4s.	10d.
£1	3s.	4d.

In the *London Evening Post*, April 27th to 30th, 1745, it is stated : " Last week a woman who keeps the Queen's Head alehouse, at Kingston, in Surrey, was ordered by the court to be ducked for scolding, and was accordingly placed in the chair and ducked in the river Thames, under Kingston Bridge, in the presence of 2000 to 3000 people."

We have previously mentioned the fact that at Leicester the cucking-stool was in use as early as 1467, and from some valuable information brought together by Mr. William Kelly, F.S.A., and included in his important local works, we learn that the last entry he has traced in the old accounts of the town is the following :

1768-9.   Paid Mr. Elliott for a Cuckstool by order
of Hall ...   .£2 0s. 0d.

Mr. Kelly refers to the scolding-cart at Leicester, and describes the culprit as seated upon it, and being drawn through the town. He found in the old accounts in 1629 an item :

Paid to Frauncis Pallmer for making two wheels and one
barr for the Scolding Cart   ...   . ijs.

Scolding-cart is another name for the tumbrel.

The latest example of Leicester cucking-stool is preserved in the local museum, and was placed there at the suggestion of Mr. Kelly.

The Leominster ducking-stool is one of the few examples still preserved. It was formerly kept in the parish church. We have an excellent drawing of it in that building from the pencil of the genial author of " Verdant Green," Cuthbert Bede. The Rev. Geo. Fyler Townsend, M.A.,

the euridite historian of Leominster, furnishes us
with some important information on this interesting relic of the olden time.   He says that it is a
machine of the simplest construction.   "It consists merely of a strong narrow under framework,
placed on four wheels, of solid wood, about four
inches in thickness, and eighteen in diameter.   At

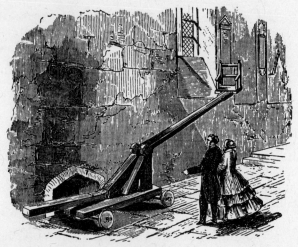

LEOMINSTER DUCKING-STOOL.

one end of this framework two upright posts,
about three feet in height, strongly embedded in
the platform, carry a long movable beam.   Each
of the arms of this beam are of equal length (13
feet), and balance perfectly from the top of the
post.   The culprit placed in the seat naturally

weighs down that one end into the water, while the other is lifted up in the air; men, however, with ropes, caused the uplifted end to rise or fall, and thus obtain a perfect see-saw. The purchase of the machine is such that the culprit can be launched forth some 16 to 18 feet into the pond or stream, while the administrators of the ducking stand on dry land. This instrument was mentioned in the ancient documents of the borough by various names, as the cucking-stoole or timbrill, or gumstole."

The latest recorded instance of the ducking-stool being used in England occurred at Leominster. In 1809, says Mr. Townsend, a woman, Jenny Pipes, alias Jane Corran, was paraded through the town on the ducking-stool, and actually ducked in the water near Kenwater Bridge, by order of the magistrates. Dr. Watling, of Kingsland, who has since that date served as bailiff to the borough, and who was present on that occasion, described the scene to Mr. Townsend. Dr. Watling gives his testimony to the desert of the punishment inflicted on this occasion, in the fact that the first words of the culprit on being unfastened from the chair were oaths and curses on the magistrates. In 1817, a woman named

Sarah Leeke was wheeled round the town in the chair, but not ducked, as the water was too low. Since this time, the use of the chair has been laid aside, and it is an object of curiosity, rather than of fear, to any of the spectators. During the recent restoration of Leominster Church, the ducking-stool was removed, repaired, and renovated by Mr. John Hungerford Arkwright, and is now kept at the borough gaol of the historically interesting town of Leominster.

The early English settlers in the United States introduced many of the manners and customs of their native land. The ducking-stool was soon brought into use. Mr. Henry M. Brooks, in his carefully written work, called "Strange and Curious Punishments," published in 1886, by Ticknor & Co., Boston, gives many important details respecting punishing scolds. At the present time, in some parts of America, scolding females are liable to be punished by means of the ducking-stool. We gather from a newspaper report that, in 1889, the grand jury of Jersey City—across the Hudson River from New York—caused a sensation by indicting Mrs. Mary Brady as a "common scold." Astonished lawyers hunted up their old books, and discovered that scolding is

still an indictable offence in New Jersey, and that
the ducking-stool is still available as a punishment for it, not having been specifically abolished
when the revised statutes were adopted. In
Delaware, the State next to the south of New
Jersey, the whipping-post is an institution, and
prisoners are sentenced to suffer at it every week.
The Common Scold Law was brought from
England to Connecticut by the Puritans and
settlers, from Connecticut they carried it with them
into New Jersey, which is incorrectly considered
a Dutch State. In closing this chapter, we may
state that a Dalziel telegram from Ottawa,
published in the London newspapers of August
8th, 1890, says that Miss Annie Pope was yesterday charged before a police magistrate, under the
provisions of an antiquated statute, for being a
" common scold." She was committed for trial at
the assizes, as the magistrate had no ducking-
stool.

The Brank, or Scold's Bridle.

THE brank was an instrument employed by our forefathers for punishing scolds. It is also sometimes called the gossip's bridle, and in the Macclesfield town records it is designated "a brydle for a curste queane." In the term "queane" we have the old English synonym for a woman ; now the chief woman, the Queen. The brank is not of such great antiquity as the duck-ing-stool, for the earliest mention of it we have been able to find in this country is in the Corporation records of Maccles-field, of the year 1623. At an earlier period, we have traces of it in Scotland. In Glasgow burgh

records, it is stated that in 1574 two scolds were condemned to be " branket." The Kirk-session records of Stirling for 1600 mention the "brankes" as a punishment for the shrew. It is generally believed that the punishment is of Continental origin.

The brank may be described simply as an iron framework; which was placed on the head, enclosing it in a kind of cage; it had in front a plate of iron, which, either sharpened or covered with spikes, was so situated as to be placed in the mouth of the victim, and if she attempted to move her tongue in any way whatever, it was certain to be shockingly injured. With the brank on her head she was conducted through the streets, led by a chain, held by one of the town's officials, an object of contempt, and subjected to the jeers of the crowd and often left to their mercy. In some towns it was the custom to chain the culprit to pillory, whipping-post, or market-cross. She thus suffered for telling her mind to some petty tyrant in office, or speaking plainly to a wrong-doer, or for taking to task a lazy, and perhaps a drunken husband.

In Yorkshire, we have only seen two branks. We give a sketch of one formerly in possession of the late Norrisson Scatcherd, F.S.A., the

historian of Morley. We believe that we are the
first to give an engraving of it. It is from the
accurate pencil of Mr. T. Tindall Wildridge, of
Hull, and is now in the Leeds Philosophical

BRANK IN THE LEEDS PHILOSOPHICAL
MUSEUM.

Museum, where it at-
tracts a considerable
share of attention. It
is one of the most
simple and harmless
examples that has
come under our notice.
Amongst the relics of
the olden time in the
Museum of the York-
shire Philosophical So-
ciety, York, is another
specimen, equally simple in its construction. It
was presented by Lady Thornton to the Society
in 1880, and near to it may be seen thumb-screws
from York Castle; leg bar, waist girdle, and wrist
shackles, worn by the notorious highwayman,
Dick Turpin, executed April 17th, 1739; and a
leg bar, worn by another notorious highwayman,
named Nevison, who suffered death on the
gallows, May 4th, 1684.

The brank which has received the greatest

attention is the one preserved in the vestry of Walton-on-Thames Parish Church. It bears the date of 1632, and the following couplet :—

" Chester presents Walton with a bridle
To curb women's tongues that talk too idle."

It is traditionally said that this brank was given to Walton Parish by a person named Chester, who had, through a gossiping and lying woman of his acquaintance, lost an estate he expected to inherit from a rich relative. We are enabled to give an illustration of the Walton brank.

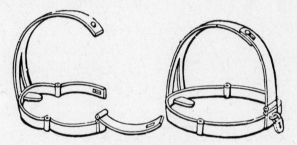

BRANK AT WALTON-ON-THAMES.

Dr. T. N. Brushfield described in an exhaustive manner all the Chester branks, in an able paper read before the Architectural, Archæological, and Historic Society of Chester, and published in 1858. We are unable to direct attention to all the branks noticed by Dr. Brushfield, but cannot refrain from presenting the following account of the one at Congleton, which is preserved in the Town Hall of that ancient borough. " It was," we are informed, " formerly in the hands of the town jailor, whose services were not infrequently called into requisition. In the old-fashioned, half-timbered houses in the borough, there was generally fixed on one side of the large open fire-places a hook, so that, when a man's wife indulged her scolding propensities, the husband sent for the town jailor to bring the bridle, and had her bridled and chained to the hook until she promised to behave herself better for the future. I have seen one of these hooks, and have often heard husbands say to their wives: ' If you don't rest with your tongue I'll send for the bridle and hook you up.' The Mayor and Justices frequently brought the instrument into use; for when women were brought before them charged with street-brawling, and insulting the constables and others while in the discharge of their duty, they have ordered them to be bridled and led through the borough by the jailor. The last time this bridle was publicly used was in 1824, when a woman was brought before the Mayor (Bulkeley Johnson, Esq.) one Monday, charged with scolding and using harsh language to the churchwardens and constables as they went, on the Sunday morning, round the town to see that all the public-houses were empty and closed during divine service. On examination, a Mr. Richard Edwards stated on oath 'that on going round the town with the churchwardens on the previous

BRANK AT CONGLETON.

day, they met the woman (Ann Runcorn) in a place near 'The Cockshoot,' and that immediately seeing them she commenced a sally of abuse, calling them all the scoundrels and rogues she could lay her tongue to; and telling them 'it would look better of them if they would look after their own houses rather than go looking after other folk's, which were far better than their own.' After other abuse of a like character, they thought it only right to apprehend her, and so brought her before the Bench on the following day. The Mayor then delivered the following sentence : 'That it is the unanimous decision of the Mayor and Justices that the prisoner (Ann Runcorn) there and then have the town's bridle for scolding women put upon her, and that she be led by the magistrate's clerk's clerk through every street in the town, as an example to all scolding women; and that the Mayor and magistrates were much obliged to the churchwardens for bringing the case before them.'" " In this case," Mr. Warrington, who furnished Dr. Brushfield with the foregoing information, adds : " I both heard the evidence and saw the decision carried out. The bridle was put on the woman, and she was then led through the town by one Prosper Haslam, the town clerk's clerk, accompanied by hundreds of the inhabitants ; and on her return to the Town Hall the bridle was taken off in the presence of the Mayor, magistrates, constables, churchwardens, and assembled inhabitants."

In Cheshire, at the present time, there are

traces of thirteen branks, and at Stockport is the most brutal example of the English branks. " It will be observed," says the local historian, Dr. Henry Heginbotham, J.P., " that the special characteristic of this brank is the peculiar construction of the tongue-plate or gag. It is about two inches long, having at the end, as may be seen in the engraving, a ball, into which is inserted a number of sharp iron pins, three on the upper surface, three on the lower, and two pointing backwards. These could not fail to pin the tongue, and effectually silence the noisiest brawler. At the fore part of the collar, there is an iron chain, with a leathern thong attached, by which the offender was led for public gaze

BRANK AT STOCKPORT.

through the market-place." It was formerly on market days exhibited in front of the house of the person who had charge of it, as a warning to scolding or swearing women. Dr. Heginbotham states that : "There is no evidence of its having been actually used for many years, but there is testimony to the fact, that within the last forty years the brank was brought to a termagant market woman, who was effectually silenced by its threatened application."

BRANK AT MACCLESFIELD.

We are indebted to Mr. Alfred Burton for a drawing of the Macclesfield brank. Dr. Brushfield describes this as "a respectable-looking brank." He tells us that "the gag is plain, and the end of it is turned down ; there is only one band which passes over the head, and is hinged to the hoops ; a temporary joint exists at the upper part, and ample provision is made for readily adjusting it to any description of head. The chain still remains attached to the hoop. About the year 1858, Mr. Swinnerton informed Dr. Brushfield that he had never seen it used, but that at the petty sessions it had often been produced *in terrorem*, to stay the volubility of a woman's tongue ; and that a threat by a magistrate to order its appliance had always proved sufficient to abate the garrulity of the most determined scold. Mr. Way, however, says that it had been used within the memory of an aged official of the municipal authorities."

Towards the close of the first quarter of the present century, the brank was last used at Altrincham. A virago, who caused her neighbours great trouble, was frequently cautioned in vain respecting her conduct, and as a last resource she was condemned to walk through the town wearing the brank. She refused to move, and it was finally decided to wheel her in a barrow through the principal streets of the town, round the market-place, and to her own home.

The punishment had the desired effect, and for the remainder of her life she kept a quiet tongue.

There are many traces of the brank in Lancashire. Mr. W. E. A. Axon informs us that his father remembers the brank being used at Manchester at the commencement of the present century. Kirkham had its brank for scolds, in addition to a ducking-stool. We find, in the same county, traces of the brank at Holme, in the Forest of Rossendale. In the accounts of the Greave for the Forest of Rossendale for 1691-2 is an entry of the true antiquarian cast :

Item, for a Bridle for scouldinge women,   ...   2s.   6d.

In "Some Obsolete Peculiarities of English Law," by Mr. William Beamont, are some interesting particulars respecting the Warrington brank. "Hanging up in our museum," says Mr. Beamont, "may be seen a representation of a withered female face wearing the brank or scold's bridle; one of which instruments, as inflexible as iron and ingenuity can make it, for keeping an unruly tongue quiet by mechanical means, hangs up beside it; and almost within the time of living memory, Cicily Pewsill, an inmate of the workhouse, and a notorious scold, was seen wearing this disagreeable head-gear in the streets of Warrington for half-an-hour or more . . . . . Cicily Pewsill's case still lingers in tradition, as the last occasion of its application in Warrington, and it will soon pass into history." According to Mr. Jewitt, "at Bolton-le-Moors, even within memory, a brank has been used as a punishment for prostitutes. The bridle was fixed in their mouths and tied at the back of their heads with gay ribbons, and thus the frail ones were paraded from the cross to the church steps and back again by the parish beadles."

Respecting the Preston brank, we find some notes in a work by Mr. W. Dobson, entitled, "Preston in the Olden Time," published in 1857. Mr. Dobson says: "The Rev. J. Clay tells me that since his connection with our House of Correction the brank was put on a woman there, but the matter coming to the knowledge of the Home Secretary, its further use was prohibited, and to make sure of the barbarous practice being discontinued the brank itself was ordered to be sent to London." A second brank was kept in the prison, principally formed of leather, but with an iron tongue-piece.

At the north country town of Morpeth a brank

is still preserved. The following is a record of its use: "Dec. 3, 1741, Elizabeth, wife of George Holborn, was punished with the branks for two hours, at the Market Cross, Morpeth, by order of Mr. Thomas Gait and Mr. George Nicholls, then bailiffs, for scandalous and opprobrious language to

BRANK AT THE MANOR HOUSE, HAMSTALL RIDWARE.

several persons in the town, as well as to the said bailiffs."

Staffordshire supplies several notable examples of the brank. They were formerly kept at Hamstall Ridware, Beaudesart, Lichfield, Walsall, and at Newcastle-under-Lyme. The branks in the two towns last named are alluded to by the celebrated Dr. Plot, the old historian of the county, in an amusing manner. "We come to the arts that respect mankind," says Plot, "amongst which, as elsewhere, the civility of precedence must be allowed to the women, and that as well in punishments as favours. For the former, whereof they have such a peculiar artifice at Newcastle [under Lyme] and Walsall for correcting of scolds, which it does, too, so effectually and so very safely, that I look upon it as much to be preferred to the cucking-stool, which not only endangers the health of the party, but also gives her tongue liberty 'twixt every dip, to neither of which is this at all liable, it being such a bridle for the tongue as not only quite deprives them of speech, but brings shame for the transgression, and humility thereupon, before 'tis taken off. Which, being an instrument scarce heard of, much less seen, I have here presented it to the reader's view [here follows a reference to a plate] as it was taken from the original one, made of iron, at Newcastle-under-Lyme, wherein the letter a shows the jointed collar that comes round the neck; b, c, the loops and staples to let it out and in, according to the bigness and

slenderness of the neck ; *d*, the jointed semicircle
that comes over the head, made forked at one end
to let through the nose, and *e*, the plate-iron that
is put into the mouth and keeps down the
tongue.   Which, being put upon the offender by
order of the magistrate, and fastened with a padlock behind, she is led through the town by an

BRANK AT LICHFIELD.

officer, to her shame, nor is it taken off until after
the party begins to show all external signs
imaginable of humiliation and amendment."   This
brank afterwards passed into the hands of Joseph
Mayer, Esq., F.S.A., founder of the Museum
at Liverpool.

In a copy of Dr. Plot's " History of Staffordshire," in the British Museum library, a marginal note bearing on this subject appears, which is supposed to be in the author's hand-writing. It reads as follows: "This bridle for the tongue seems to be very ancient, being mentioned by an ancient English poet, I think Chaucer, *quod vide:*

> But for my daughter Julian,
> I would she were well bolted with a Bridle,
> That leaves her work to play the clack,
> And let's her wheel stand idle,
> For it serves not for she-ministers,
> Farriers nor Furriers,
> Cobblers nor Button-makers,
> To descant on the Bible.

It is pleasing to record the fact that there is only trace of one brank belonging to Derbyshire —a circumstance which speaks well for its men and women. The latter have for a long period borne exemplary characters. Philip Kinder, in the preface of his projected "History of Derbyshire," written about the middle of the seventeenth century, alludes to them. "The country-women here," says Kinder, "are chaste and sober, and very diligent in their housewifery; they hate idleness, love and obey their husbands; only in some of the great towns many of the seeming sanctificators used to follow the Presbyterian gang, and on a lecture day put on their best rayment,

and doo hereby take occasion to goo a gossipping.
Your merry wives of Bentley will sometimes look
in ye glass, chirpe a cupp merrily, yet not
indecently. In the Peak they are much given to
dance after the bagpipes—almost every towne hath
a bagpipe in it." In the *Reliquary* for October,

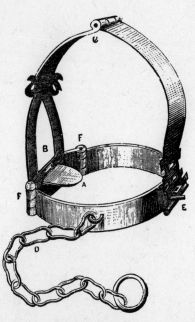

CHESTERFIELD BRANK.

1860, we have an account of the Derbyshire
brank. The editor, Mr. Llewellynn Jewitt, says:
"The Chesterfield brank, for the first time engraved, is a remarkably good example, and has
the additional interest of bearing a date. It is

nine inches in height, and six inches and three-quarters across the hoop. It consists of a hoop of iron, hinged on either side and fastening behind, and a band, also of iron, passing over the head from back to front, and opening in front to admit the nose of the woman whose misfortune it was to wear it. The mode of putting it on would be thus : the brank would be opened by throwing back the sides of the hoop, and the hinder part of the band by means of the hinges, c, f, f. The constable, or other official, would then stand in front of his victim, and force the knife, or plate, a, into her mouth, the divided band passing on either side of her nose, which would protrude through the opening, b. The hoop would then be closed behind, the band brought down from the top to the back of the head, and fastened down upon it, at e, and thus the cage would at once be firmly and immovably fixed so long as her tormentors might think fit. On the left side is a chain, d, one end of which is attached to the hoop, and at the other end is a ring, by which the victim was led, or by which she was, at pleasure, attached to a post or wall. On front of the brank are the initials " t.c.," and the date " 1688 "—the year of the " Glorious Revolution "—the year of all years, memorable in the annals of Chesterfield and the little village of Whittington, closely adjoining, in which the Revolution was planned. Strange that an instrument of brutal and tyrannical torture should be made and used at Chesterfield, at the same moment that the people should be plotting for freedom at the same place. The brank was formerly in the old poor-house at Chesterfield, and came into the hands of Mr. Weale, the assistant Poor-law Commissioner, who presented it to Lady Walsham. It is (August, 1860) still in the hands of Sir John Walsham, Bart., and the drawing from which the accompanying woodcut is executed, and kindly made and furnished to me by Miss Dulcy Bell, Sir John's sister-in-law."

The Leicester brank is similar to the one at Chesterfield. At the back of the hoop is a chain about twelve inches long. It was formerly kept in the Leicester borough gaol.

In the year 1821, Judge Richardson gave orders for a brank to be destroyed which was kept ready and most probably frequently used at the County Hall, Nottingham. We gather from a note furnished by Mr. J. Potter Briscoe a curious circumstance in connection with this brank—

that it was used to subdue the unruly tongues of
the sterner sex, as well as those of noisy females.

James Brodie, a blind
beggar, who was executed
on the 15th July, 1799,
for the murder of his
boy-guide, in the Nottingham Forest, was the last
person punished with the
brank. During his im-
prisonment, prior to exe-

LEICESTER BRANK.

cution, he was so noisy that the brank was called
into requisition, to do what he refused to do himself, namely, to hold his tongue.

BRANK FORMERLY IN POSSESSION OF MR. CARRINGTON.

Here is a picture of a brank formerly in the

possession of the late Mr. F. A. Carrington, the
well-known antiquary. It is supposed to belong
to the period of William III. Mr. Carrington
could not give any history of this curious relic of
the olden time.

At Doddington Park, Lincolnshire, a brank is
preserved, and is of a decidedly foreign appearance. It will be noticed that it bears some

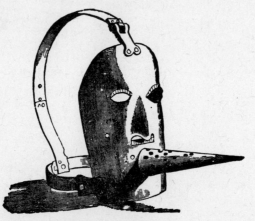

BRANK AT DODDINGTON PARK.

resemblance to the peculiar long-snouted visor of
the bascinets, occasionally worn in the reign of
Richard II. No historical particulars are known
respecting this grotesque brank.

In the Ashmolean Museum at Oxford, a curious
brank may be seen. It is not recorded in the
catalogue of the collection by whom it was

presented, or where it was previously used; it is described as " a gag or brank, formerly used with the ducking-stool, as a punishment for scolds." It will be noticed that a chain is attached to the front of this brank, so that the poor unfortunate woman, in addition to being gagged, had the

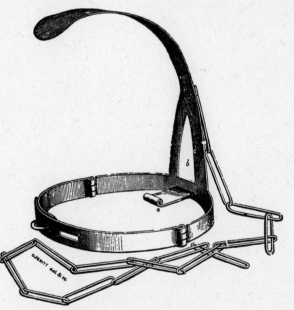

BRANK IN THE ASHMOLEAN MUSEUM.

mortification of being led by the nose through the town. The gag is marked a, and b is the aperture for the nose.

A curious engine of torture may be seen in the Ludlow Museum, and of which we give an

illustration. It belongs to a class of engines
far more formidable than branks. A description of this head-piece appears in the *Archæological Journal* for September, 1856, from the
pen of Mr. W. J. Bernard Smith. "The power-
ful screwing apparatus," says Mr. Smith, " seems

calculated to force
the iron mask with
torturing effect upon
the brow of the vic-
tim; there are no
eye-holes, but con-
cavities in their
places, as though to
allow for the start-
ing of the eye-balls
under violent pres-
sure. There is a
strong bar with a

ENGINE OF TORTURE IN THE LUDLOW
MUSEUM.

square hole, evidently intended to fasten the criminal against a wall, or perhaps to the pillory; and
I have heard it said that these instruments were
used to keep the head steady during the inflic-
tion of branding." A curious instrument of
punishment, belonging to the same class as
that at Ludlow, is described at some length,

with an illustration in "Worcester in Olden Times," by John Noake (London, 1849). The picture and description have been frequently reproduced.

Several Shropshire branks remain at the present time. The one at Shrewsbury does not appear to be of any great antiquity. Its form is simple and its character harmless. We give an illustration of it from "The Obsolete Punishments of Shropshire," by S. Meeson Morris,

SHREWSBURY BRANK.

contributed to the pages of the transactions of a local antiquarian society. "This bridle was," says Mr. Morris, "at one time, in constant use in Shrewsbury, and there are those yet living whose memories are sufficiently good to carry them back to the days when the effects of the application of the brank in question were to be seen, rather than, as now imagined." The year cannot be ascertained when this brank was first

worn, but it is known to have been last used in
1846. We learn from Mr. Morris, in that year
"a woman, then a resident in Frankwell, was
ordered to undergo this peculiar punishment, for
having made use of abusive and opprobrious
epithets to a neighbour, and she suffered
accordingly. This woman is still living, and she
refers to the occasion in question with evident
pride, rather than evincing any signs of
humiliation for the ignominious position in which
she was placed. Probably her fellow-townspeople
had, by the time she suffered, become aware of
the fact that so barbarous a punishment was not
altogether suited to the spirit of the age, and
received her with expressions of sympathy rather
than with jeers of laughter." At Oswestry are
two branks, one belonging to the Corporation
and the other in the storeroom of the Workhouse.
The Rector of Whitchurch has in his possession
a brank, which was formerly used by the town
and union authorities. At Market Drayton
are two branks : one is the property of the Lord
of the Manor, and the other formerly belonged to
the Dodcot Union. The Market Drayton brank,
and also the one at Whitchurch, have on each a
revolving wheel at the end of the gag or tongue-

plate. In bygone times, the brank was frequently used for correcting unmanageable paupers.

In the Museum, at Edinburgh, of the Society of Antiquaries of Scotland, is a brank said to be from a town in East Fifeshire, having a rowel-shaped gag. In the year 1560, it was decided by the Town Council of Edinburgh, that all persons found guilty of blasphemy should be punished by the iron brank. Dr. Charles Rogers, in his "Social Life in Scotland," has numerous references to the brank. In North Britain, it appears to have been much used for punishing persons guilty of fornication. On the 7th October, says Dr. Rogers, the Kirk-Session of Canongate sentenced David Persoun, convicted of

BRANK IN THE ANTIQUARIAN MUSEUM, EDINBURGH.

fornication, to be " brankit for four hours," while his associate in guilt, Isobel Mountray, was "banisit the gait," that is, expelled from the parish. Only a week previously, the same Kirk-

Session had issued a proclamation that all women found guilty of fornication " be brankit six houris at the croce."

In 1848 was discovered, behind the oak panelling in one of the rooms of the ancient mansion of the Earls of Moray, in the Canongate, Edinburgh, a brank, of which a picture is given in Dr. Daniel Wilson's " Prehistoric Annals of Scotland," vol. ii., p. 520. It is one of the more harmless, and not calculated to wound the mouth of the person wearing it.

We close this chapter by directing attention to the Bishop's brank, kept at St. Andrews, respecting which a singular story is told. A woman in a humble walk of life, named Isabel Lindsay, stood up in the parish church of St. Andrews, during the time of divine service, when Archbishop Sharp was preaching, and declared that when he was a college student he was guilty of an illicit amour with her. She was arrested for this statement, and brought before the Kirk-Session, and by its members sentenced " to appear for a succession of Sundays on the repentance stool, wearing the brank."

The Pillory.

THE pillory may be traced back to a remote period in England and in other European countries. The mention of it calls to remembrance the names of many who figure in the annals of our country, embracing not a few of the noblest and the best; but there are those of others which, for the credit of the nation, we would gladly allow to sink into oblivion. Round it gathers tragedy and comedy, and, altogether, its history is of interest and importance.

In this country, in bygone days, the pillory was a familiar sight, and, perhaps, no engine of punishment was more generally employed. Where there was a market, a pillory might be seen, for the local authorities, neglecting to keep it ready for immediate use as occasion might require, ran the risk of forfeiting the right of holding a market. Lords of Manors, in addition to having the right of a pillory, usually had a ducking-stool and gallows. Thomas de Chaworth, in the reign of

Edward III., made a claim of a park, and the right of free warren, at Alfreton, with the privilege of having a gallows, tumbrel, and pillory.

In the middle ages, frequently a pillory, whipping-post, and stocks were combined, and

PILLORY, WHIPPING-POST, AND STOCKS, WALLINGFORD.

we give a picture of a good example from Wallingford, Berkshire. It will be observed that they are planned to hold four delinquents, namely, one in the pillory, one at the whipping-post, and two in the stocks. They stood near the town hall, in the market-place, down to about the year 1830, when the pillory and whipping-post were taken down. The stocks remained for a few years longer to remind the tippler of his fate, if he overstepped the bounds of temperance and was caught drunk. In course of time they fell into disuse, and were finally presented by the Corporation to Mr. J. Kirby Hedges, of Wallingford Castle, the historian of the ancient town. He informs us that there was a pillory at Wallingford in 1231, and probably earlier.

A good representation of the pillory formerly much used is furnished in a cut of Robert Ockam, undergoing part of his sentence for perjury, in the reign of Henry VIII. In the year 1543, Ockam, with two other criminals mounted on horseback, with papers on their heads, and their faces towards the tails of the horses, had to ride about Windsor, Newbury and Reading,  and stand in the pillory of each of the three towns.

We give a view of an ancient pillory which formerly stood in the market-place of the village of Paulmy, in Touraine. It is copied from a picture of the Castle of Paulmy in *Cosmographie Universelle*, 1575. It will be observed that it is

PILLORY FOR A NUMBER OF PERSONS.

planned for holding a number of offenders at the same time. This form of pillory was not generally used. It was usually much simpler in construction, and frequently was not a permanent structure.

The following are some of the offences for which persons have been condemned to this species of discipline : Bakers for default of weight (without remittance " for gold or silver.") Brewers for not keeping the assize. Butchers for exposing unwholesome meat, which was burned under their noses. Adulterers and fore-stallers, dice coggers, forgers, cut-purses, liars and libellers, and passers-off of latten rings for gold. Ten bakers, in the year 1327, were pilloried for having trap-doors on their moulding-boards, through which confederates abstracted part of the dough. Those bakers beneath whose table any dough was found, were adorned in the pillory by having some of the stolen property hung round their necks ! In 1364, John de Hakford, for telling a friend that there were ten thousand men ready to rise and slay the chief men of London, was sentenced to be imprisoned for a year and a day, and to stand in the pillory for three hours once every quarter "without hood or girdle, barefoot and unshod, with a whetstone hung by a chain from his neck, and lying on his breast, it being marked with the words, *A False Liar*, and there shall be a pair of trumpets trumpeting before him on his way." A man, in the year

1371, was put into the pillory for saying that
aliens might sell as freely as freemen. In 1379,
a fellow suffered the pillory for taking false
invitations to dine and receiving gratuities for the
same. In 1382, a maltman was pilloried and
burdened with a whetstone for saying the mayor
had been sent to the tower. It was in the same
year a conjuror was sent to the pillory for causing,
by his divinations, a woman to be accused of a
theft; a quack also suffered the same punishment
for affecting to cure a sick woman by wrapping a
piece of parchment about her neck. A gentleman, in 1552, was "set on" the Cheapside pillory
for fraud, with his ears nailed to it, and, when the
prescribed period being fulfilled, " he would not
rent his eare, one of the bedles slitted yt upwards
with a penkniffe to loose yt." In some cases the
nose was slit, the face branded with letters, and
one or both ears cut off. During the trembling
reign of the ill-starred Lady Jane Grey, a
vintner's drawer had both ears nailed to the
pillory, by commandment of the Privy Council,
and cut clean off, " for seditious and trayterous
words speaking of the Queene yesternight." A
trumpeter blew a blast to announce the perform-
ance of the act, while during the actual

" cuttinge," his enormity was proclaimed by a herald. Later, Queen Mary's reign was diversified by like exhibitions. In 1556, one offender was brought " from Westminster Hall, ridinge with his face to the horse tayle, with a paper on his head, to the Stenderd in Cheape, and there set on the pillorie, and then burned with a hott iron on both his cheeks with two letters (F. and A.) for false accusinge of the Court of the Common Place for treason."

Stow, in his " Survey of London," supplies a description of the Cornhill pillory, and gives particulars of the crimes for which it was brought into requisition. After adverting to the making of a strong prison of timber, called a cage, and fixing upon it a pair of stocks for night-walkers, he next tells us: " On the top of the cage was placed a pillory, for the punishment of bakers offending in the assize of bread; for millers stealing of corn at the mill; for bawds, scolds, and other offenders." As in the year 1486, the seventh of Edward IV., divers persons, being common jurors, such as at assizes, were forsworn for rewards or favour of parties, were judged to ride from Newgate to the pillory of Cornhill, with mitres of paper on their heads, there to stand, and from thence again to Newgate ; and this judgment was given by the Mayor of London. In the year 1509, the first of Henry VIII., Darby, Smith, and Simson, ringleaders of false inquests in London, rode about the city with their faces to the horses' tails, and papers on their heads, and were set on the pillory in Cornhill, and after brought again to Newgate, where they died for very shame, saith Robert Fabian.

A curious note, relating to this topic, appears in the " Journal of Henry Machyn, Citizen of London," published by the Camden Society.   It is stated that, on the 1st July, 1552, there was a man and woman on the pillory in Cheapside : the man sold pots of strawberries, the which were not half full, but filled with fern. On the 30th May, 1554, two persons were set on the pillory, a man and a woman ; but the woman had her ear nailed to the pillory for speaking of false lies and rumours. The man was for seditious and slanderous words.

An instance of great severity is recorded in 1621, when Edward Floyd was convicted of having used slighting expressions concerning the king's son-in-law, the Elector Palatine, and his wife. The sentence was given as follows : (1)

Not to bear arms as a gentleman, nor be a competent witness in any Court of Justice. (2) To ride with his face to a horse's tail, to stand in the pillory, and have his ears nailed, etc. (3) To be whipped at the cart's tail. (4) To be fined £5,000. (5) To be perpetually imprisoned in Newgate. It was questioned whether Floyd, being a gentleman, should be whipped, and have his ears nailed. It was agreed by a majority that he should be subject to the former, but not to the latter. He stood two hours in the pillory, and had his forehead branded.

Pepys, writing in his diary under date of March 26th, 1664, relates that he had been informed by Sir W. Batten that "some 'prentices, being put in the pillory to-day for beating of their masters, or such-like thing, in Cheapside, a company of 'prentices came and rescued them, and pulled down the pillory ; and they being set up again, did the like again." We may infer, from the foregoing and other facts that have come down to us respecting the London apprentices, that they were a power in bygone times, doing very much as they pleased.

We are enabled, by the courtesy of Messrs. W. & R. Chambers, to reproduce from their

"Book of Days" an excellent illustration of Oates in the pillory (from a contemporary print). "Found guilty," says the writer in the "Book of

OATES IN THE PILLORY (FROM A CONTEMPORARY PRINT).

Days," "of perjury on two separate indictments, the inventor of the Popish Plot was condemned, in 1685, to public exposure on three consecutive days. The first day's punishment, in Palace Yard, nearly cost the criminal his life; but his partisans mustered in such force in the city, on the succeeding day, that they were able to upset the pillory, and nearly succeeded in rescuing their idol from the hands of the authorities. According to his sentence, Oates was to stand every year of his life in the pillory, on five different days: before the gate of Westminster Hall, on the 9th August; at Charing Cross on the 10th; at the Temple on the 11th; at the Royal Exchange on the 2nd September; and at Tyburn on the 24th April; but, fortunately for the infamous creature, the Revolution deprived his determined enemies of power, and turned the criminal into a pensioner of Government."

It was formerly a common custom to put persons in the pillory during the time of public market. We may name, as an example, a case occurring at Canterbury, in 1524. A man was set up in the pillory, which was in the Market Place, and bearing on his head a paper inscribed, "This is a false, perjured, and forsworn man." He was confined in the pillory until the market

was over, and then led to Westgate and thrust
out of the town, still wearing the paper. " If he
be proud," says an old writer, " he may go home
and shew himself among his neighbours."

The Corporation accounts of Newcastle-on-
Tyne contain, among other curious items, the
following :

1561.—Paid to the Gawyng Aydon, for squrgyn a
    boye about the town, and for settying a man
    in the pallerye, two days ... ...   16d.
1562.—Paid for a tre to the pillyre   ... ...   5s.
1574.—Paid to Charles Shawe, for charges in carry-
    inge the man to Durham that stode in the
    pillarye, and was skrougide aboute the town
    at Mr. Maior's commandement... ... ...   3s.
1593.—Paide for a Papist which studd in the pillerie
    for abusing Oure Majestie by slanderous
    woordes... ... ...   4d.
1594.—Paide for 4 papers to 4 folke which was sett on
    the pillorie ... ...   16d.
    Paide Ro. Musgrave for takinge paines to
    sett them upp   ... ...   8d.

The " papers " above mentioned were for the
purpose of proclaiming to the world at large the
nature of the bearer's offence.

At Hull, in the year 1556, the town ordinances
were revised and proclaimed " in the Market
Place, in the market-time, according to the yearly
custom." The twenty-third rule runs as follows :
" That no person whomsoever, presume to take

down and carry away, any brick or stones off or from the town's walls, upon pain for every default to be set upon the pillory, and to pay, for a fine, to the town's chamber, forty shillings." We may infer, from the foregoing, that the town's walls, both the original stone portion of Edward I., and the later addition of brick, were in a state of demolition. In 1559, the aldermen of Hull were directed to take account of " all vagabonds, idle persons, sharpers, beggars, and such like; " and, doubtless, not a few of the persons included under these wide definitions would come to the pillory, for the aldermen were ordered to " punish them severely; " and, as the punishments of Hull were largely in fines, Mr. Wildridge, author of " Old and New Hull," suggests the moneyless classes of persons above-named would be most economically and severely dealt with by pillorying. About 1813, a man, for keeping a disreputable house, was placed in the pillory erected in the Market-Place.

At Preston, Lancashire, in 1814, a man about sixty years of age was pilloried for a similar offence, and it is said that he was the last person punished in this manner in the town.

Mr. John Nicholson, author of " Folk Lore of

East Yorkshire," says that the pillory at Driffield was movable, and when in use stood in the Market Place, near the Cross Keys Hotel. The last occupants, a man and a woman, were pilloried together about 1810, for fortune-telling. The Bridlington pillory stood in the Market Place, opposite the Corn Exchange. It was taken down about 1835, and lay some time in Well Lane, but it finally disappeared, and was probably chopped up for firewood. Before its removal, there was affixed to it a bell, which was rung to regulate the market hours. Mischievous youths, however, often rang it, so it was taken down in 1810, and kept at a house down a court, known as Pillory Bell Yard.

Mr. W. E. A. Axon, the well-known Lancashire author and antiquary, kindly supplies the following particulars respecting the Manchester pillory : " The earliest notice of the pillory in Manchester," says Mr. Axon, " is the Court Leet Records, 8th April, 1624, when the jury referred the erection of a ' gibbett' to the discretion of the Steward and the Boroughreeve. Some delay must have occurred, for on the 8th April, 1625, ' the jurye doth order that the constables for this yeare, att the charges of the inhabitants, shall

cause to bee erected and sett vp a sufficient
gibbett or pilorye for the vse of this towne, in
some convenient place about the Markett Crosse,
and to take to them the advice of Mr. Steward
and the Bororeve. This to be done before the
xxiiijth day of August next, subpena xx^{s}.' This

MANCHESTER PILLORY.

threat of a penalty was effective, and the careful
scribe notes *factum est*. The convenient place
was in the market-place, close to the stocks. The
pillory remained, more or less in use, until 1816,
when it was removed. Barritt, the antiquary,
made a drawing of it, which has been engraved.

It was jocularly styled the 'tea table,' and was used as a whipping place also. In the present century, it was not a permanent fixture, but a movable structure, set up when required. One pilloried individual, grimly jesting at his own sorrows, told an inquiring friend that he was celebrating his nuptials with Miss Wood, and that his neighbour, whom the beadle was whipping, had come to dance at the wedding. During the Civil War, there was a pillory for the special benefit of the soldiers, and it was removed from the Corn Market in 1651."

The Rev. J. Charles Cox, LL.D., in his " Three Centuries of Derbyshire Annals," adverts to the general employment of the pillory in bygone times. " The two or three calendars," says Dr. Cox, " of prisoners of Elizabethan days pertaining to Derbyshire that have come down to our times, are a proof of its frequent application. Five persons on one occasion, and nine on another, were condemned to exposure in the pillory at Derby, previous to a short period of imprisonment. At the summer assizes, 1726, John Clowne, convicted of a misdemeanor, is ordered to be set in the pillory next market-day, at Derby, between the hours of eleven and one, for the space of one hour, and to suffer three months' imprisonment."

The Rye pillory still remains, and we give a picture of it from a photograph taken for the late Llewellynn Jewitt, F.S.A. The last time it

PILLORY AT RYE.

was used was in the year 1813, when a publican was put in it for aiding the escape of General Philippon, a French prisoner of war, who had been brought to the town. The pillory was erected on the beach, and the face of the culprit, when undergoing the punishment, turned to the

coast of France. Mr. Holloway, the historian of
Rye, supplied Mr. Jewitt with some interesting
particulars respecting this pillory. " It measures,"
says Mr. Holloway, " about six feet in height, by
four in width. It consists of two up-posts affixed
to a platform, and has two transverse rails, the
upper one of which is divided horizontally, and
has a hinge to admit of the higher portion being
lifted, so as to allow of the introduction of the
culprit's head and hands. Through the platform
and the lower rail there are round perforations,
into which, when the instrument was in
requisition, an upright bar, probably of iron, was
introduced, so as to allow the pillory, with its
unfortunate tenant, to be turned bodily round at
pleasure."

It will not be without interest to reproduce,
from contemporary newspapers and other publica-
tions, particulars of persons being pilloried. We
may learn, from a report in *Fog's Weekly Journal*,
for June 12th, 1731, to what a fearful extent old-
time punishments were carried. It is stated that on
" Thursday, Japhet Cook, *alias* Sir Peter Stringer,
who was, some time since, convicted of forging
deeds of conveyance of two thousand acres of land
belonging to Mr. Garbett and his wife, lying in

the Parish of Claxton, in the County of Essex, was brought, by the keeper of the King's Bench, to Charing Cross, where he stood in the pillory from twelve to one, pursuant to his sentence. The time being near expired, he was set on a chair on the pillory, when the hangman, dressed like a butcher, came to him, and, with a knife like a gardener's pruning-knife, cut off his ears, and, with a pair of scissors, slit both his nostrils : all which Cook bore with great patience ; but, at the searing, with hot irons, of his right nostril, the pain was so violent that he got up from his chair. His left nostril was not seared, so he went from the pillory bleeding."

A remarkable scene at the pillory is recorded in the pages of the "Annual Register," under date of June 25th, 1759 : " Samuel Scrimshaw and James Ross," it is stated, " stood in the pillory for sending a threatening letter to extort a large sum of money from Humphrey Morrice, Esq., and were severely pelted by the populace ; but one of the sheriff's officers, having received an affront by being too near the pillory, drew his sword, and fell pell-mell among the thickest of the people, cutting his way indiscriminately through men, women, and children. This diverted the fury of the mob from the criminals to the officer, who, not being able to stand against such numbers, made good his retreat to an adjoining alley, where not above two or three could press upon him at a time, and so escaped." It will be gathered from the following report culled from the *Craftsman*, of November 25th, 1786, that large guards of constables attended to keep order when persons were pilloried. "Yesterday," says the report, "at twelve o'clock, Mr. A——, the attorney, was brought from Newgate in a hackney-coach, and put into the pillory, which was fixed in the middle of Palace Yard, opposite Westminster Hall gate, and stood for one hour. He was attended by the sheriffs, under-sheriffs, and two city marshals, and about six hundred constables, who kept everything quiet. It is supposed that upwards of four thousand people were assembled; but, owing to the sheriffs and other officers keeping a continual look-out, and riding on horse-back about Palace Yard the whole time, not any disturbance happened. He was then put into a hackney-coach, and carried back to Newgate."

The following is extracted from the *Morning Herald*, of January 28th, 1804 : " The enormity of Thomas Scott's offence, in endeavouring to accuse Captain Kennah, a respectable officer, together with his servant, of robbery, having attracted much public notice, his conviction, that followed the attempt, could not but be gratifying to all lovers of justice. Yesterday, the culprit underwent a part of his punishment: he was placed in the pillory, at Charing Cross, for one hour. On his first appearance, he was greeted by a large mob with a discharge of small shot, such as rotten eggs, filth, and dirt from the streets, which was followed up by dead cats, rats, etc., which had been collected in the vicinity of the Metropolis by the boys in the morning. When he was taken away to Cold Bath Fields, to which place he was sentenced for twelve months, the mob broke the windows of the coach, and would have proceeded to violence had not the police officers been at hand."

In the "Annual Register," under date of September 27th, 1810, are given the following particulars of a number of persons being placed in the pillory at the same time: "Cooke, the publican of the 'Swan,' in Vere Street, and five other of the eleven miscreants convicted of detestable practices, stood in the pillory in the

Haymarket, opposite to Panton Street. Such was the degree of popular indignation excited against these wretches, and such was the general eagerness to witness their punishment, that by ten in the morning all the windows, and even the roofs of the houses, were crowded with persons of both sexes; and every coach, waggon, hay-cart, dray, and other vehicle, which blocked up a great part of the streets, were crowded with spectators. The sheriffs, attended by the two city marshals, with an immense number of constables, accompanied the procession of the prisoners from Newgate, where they set out in the transport caravan, and proceeded through Fleet Street and the Strand; and the prisoners were hooted and pelted the whole way by the populace. At one o'clock, four of the culprits were fixed in the pillory, erected for, and accommodated to the occasion with, two additional wings, one being allotted to each criminal. Immediately a new torrent of popular vengeance poured upon them from all sides—blood, garbage, and ordure from the slaughter-house, diversified with dead cats, turnips, potatoes, addled eggs, and other missiles, to the last moment. Two wings of the pillory were then taken off to place Cooke and Amos in,

who, although they came in for the second course,
had no reason to complain of short allowance.
The vengeance of the crowd pursued them back to
Newgate, and the caravan was filled with mud
and ordure. No interference from the sheriffs
and police officers could restrain the popular rage;
but, notwithstanding the immensity of the multi-
tude, no accident of any note occurred."

The famous Lord Thurlow was eloquent for the
preservation of the pillory, which he called "the
restraint against licentiousness, provided by the
wisdom of past ages." This was in a case against
the Rev. Horne Tooke, who, escaped with a fine
of £200. Of others, who have spoken for and
against it, may be mentioned Lord Macclesfield,
who, in 1719, condemned it as a punishment for
State criminals. In 1791, Pitt claimed to have
dissuaded the Government from its too frequent
use, as had Burke. In 1812, Lord Ellenborough
sentenced a blasphemer to the pillory for two
hours once a month, for eighteen months. In
1814, again, he ordered Lord Cochrane, the
famous sea-fighter of Brasque Roads fame, to be
pilloried for conspiring with others to spread false
news. But his colleague, Sir Francis Burdett,
declared that he would stand by his side in the

pillory regardless of consequences. In the then state of public opinion, the Government declined to undertake the responsibility, and this punishment was waived.

It was no uncommon circumstance for the offenders to be killed on the pillory, by the pelting which they were subjected to by the fury of the crowd. In 1731, a professional witness, *i.e.*, one who for the reward offered for the conviction of criminals, would swear falsely against them, was sentenced to the pillory of Seven Dials, where, so bitter were the populace against him that they pelted him to death. The coroner's jury returned a verdict of "wilful murder by persons unknown." In 1756, the drovers of Smithfield pelted two perjured thief-catchers so violently that one died; in 1763, a man died from a like cause, at Southwark; in 1780, a coachman died from injuries before his time had expired.

An amusing anecdote is related, bearing upon a pillory accident. "A man," says Chambers' "Book of Days," "being condemned to the pillory in or about Elizabeth's time, the footboard on which he was placed proved to be rotten, and down it fell, leaving him hanging by the neck, in danger of his life. On being liberated, he brought an action against the town for the insufficiency of its pillory, and recovered damages."

In the year 1812, the pillory ceased to be employed for punishing persons, except in cases of perjury, and for this crime a man was put in the pillory in 1830. The pillory, in the year 1837, was abolished by Act of Parliament.

The next chapter furnishes further particulars respecting the pillory. In bygone times it was very generally used for punishing authors.

Punishing Authors and Burning Books.

LITERARY annals contain many records of the punishments of authors. The Greeks and Romans frequently brought writers into contempt by publicly burning their books. In England, in years agone, it was a common practice to place in the pillory authors who presumed to write against the reigning monarch, or on political and religious subjects which were not in accord with the opinions of those in power. The public hangman was often directed to make bonfires of the works of offending authors. At Athens, the common crier was instructed to burn all the prohibited works of Pythagoras which could be found. It is well known that Numa did much to build up the glory of Rome. It was he who gave to his countrymen the ceremonial laws of religion, and it was under his rule that they enjoyed the blessings of peace. His death was keenly felt by a grateful people, and he was honoured with a grand and costly funeral. In his grave were found some of his writings, which were contrary to his religious teaching ; and the fact being made known to the Senate, an order was made directing the manuscripts to be consumed by fire. In the days of Augustus, no less than twenty thousand volumes were consigned on one occasion to the flames. The works of Labienus were amongst those which were burnt. It was a terrible blow to the author and some of his friends. Cassius Severus, when he heard the sentence pronounced, exclaimed in a loud voice that they must burn him also, for he had learnt all the books by heart. It was the death-blow to Labienus ; he repaired to the tomb of his fore-fathers, refused food, and pined away. It is asserted that he was buried alive. At Constantinople, Leo I. caused two hundred thousand books to be consumed by fire.

The Bible did not escape the flames. It is stated by Eusebius that, by the direction of Dioclesian, the Scriptures were burnt. According to Foxe, the well-known writer on the martyrs, on May, 1531, Bishop Stokesley "caused all the New Testament of Tindal's translation, and many other books which he had bought, to be openly burnt in St. Paul's churchyard." It was there that the Bishop of Rochester in a sermon denounced Martin Luther and all his works. He spoke of all who kept his books as accursed. Not a few of the condemned works were publicly burnt during the delivery of the sermon.

A man named Stubbs, in the reign of Queen Elizabeth, lost his hand for writing a pamphlet of Radical tendencies.

A gentleman named Collingbourne, wrote the following couplet respecting Gatesby, Ratcliff, and Lovel giving their advice to Richard III., whose crest, it will be remembered, was a white boar :

> " The cat, the rat, and Lovel our dog,
> Rule all England under a hog."

He was executed on Tower Hill for writing the foregoing lines. After " having been hanged," it is recorded, " he was cut down immediately, and his entrails were then extracted and thrown into the fire ; and all this was so speedily performed that," Stow says, " when the executioner pulled out his heart, he spoke, and said, ' Jesus, Jesus.'"

It is generally understood that Christopher Marlow translated, as a college exercise, " Amores of Ovid." It was a work of unusual ability ; but did not, however, meet with the approval of

Archbishop Whitgift and Bishop Bancroft. In consequence, in June, 1599, all copies were ordered to be burnt. A few escaped the fire, and are now very valuable. Milton's books were burnt by the common hangman, on August 27th, 1659.

Authors and publishers were often nailed by the ears to the pillory, and when ready to be set at liberty the ears would frequently be cut off, and left on the post of the pillory. A farce called " The Patron," by Foote, contains allusions to the practice. Puff advises Dactyl to write a satire. To the suggestion replies Dactyl: " Yes, and so get cropped for libel." Puff answers him: " Cropped! aye, and the luckiest thing that could happen you! Why, I would not give twopence for an author who is afraid of his ears! Writing—writing is, as I may say, Mr. Dactyl, a sort of warfare, and none can be victor that can be least afraid of a scar. Why, zooks, sir! I never got salt to my porridge till I mounted at the Royal Exchange; and that was the making of me. Then my name made a noise in the world. Talk of forked hills and Helicon! Romance and fabulous stuff, the true Castalian stream is a shower of eggs, and a pillory the poet's Parnassus." In 1630, Dr. Leighton, a clergyman, and father of the celebrated archbishop of that name, was tried and found guilty of printing a work entitled, " Zion's Plea against Prelacy," in which he called bishops men of blood, ravens, and magpies, and pronounced the institution of Episcopacy to be satanical; he called the Queen a daughter of Heth, and even commanded the murder of Buckingham. His sentence was a hard one, and consisted of a fine of £10,000. He was also degraded the ministry, pilloried, branded, and whipped; an ear was cropped off, and his nostril slit. After enduring these punishments, he was sent to the Fleet Prison. At the end of the week, he underwent a second course of cruelty, and was consigned to prison for life. After eleven weary years passed in prison, Leighton was liberated, the House of Commons having reversed his sentence. He was told that his mutilation and imprisonment had been illegal! At this period in our history, a book or pamphlet could not be printed without a license from the Archbishop of Canterbury, the Bishop of London, or the authorities of the two universities. Only authorised printers were permitted to set up

printing presses in the City of London. Any
one printing without the necessary authority
subjected himself to the risk of being placed in
the pillory and whipped through the City.

Liburn and Warton disregarded the foregoing
order, and printed and published libellous and
seditious works. They refused to appear before
the court where such offences were tried. The
authorities found them guilty, and fined each man
£500, and ordered them to be whipped from
Fleet Prison to the pillory at Westminster. The
sentence was carried out on April the 18th, 1638.
Liburn appears to have been a man of dauntless
courage, and when in the pillory, he gave away
copies of his obnoxious works to the crowd, and
addressed them on the tyranny of his persecutors.
He was gagged to stop his speech.

William· Prynne lost his ears for writing
" Historic-Mastix : the Player's Scourge, or
Actor's Tragedie " (1633). His pillory experi-
ences were of the most painful character.

According to an entry in the annals of Hull, in
the year 1645, all the books of Common Prayer
were burned by the Parliamentary soldiers, in
the market-place.

One of Mr. C. H. Spurgeon's predecessors,

named Benjamin Keach, a Baptist Minister, of Winslow, in the County of Bucks, issued a work entitled, "The Child's Instructor; or, a New and Easy Primmer." The book was regarded as seditious, and the authorities had him tried for

BENJAMIN KEACH IN THE PILLORY

writing and publishing it, at the Aylesbury Assizes, on the 8th October, 1664. The judge passed on him the following sentence:

"Benjamin Keach, you are here convicted of writing and publishing a seditious and scandalous Book, for which the Court's judgment is this, and the Court doth award, That you shall go to gaol for a fortnight, without bail or mainprise ; and the next Saturday to stand upon the pillory at Ailsbury for the space of two hours, from eleven o'clock to one, with a Paper upon your head with this inscription, *For writing, printing and publishing a schismatical book, intitled, The Child's Instructor, or a new and easy Primmer.* And the next Thursday so stand in the same manner, and for the same time in the market of Winslow ; and there your book shall be openly burnt before your face by the common hangman, in disgrace to you and your doctrine. And you shall forfeit to the King's Majesty the sum of £20 and shall remain in goal until you find sureties for your good behaviour and appearance at the next assizes, there to renounce your doctrine, and to make such public submission as shall be enjoined you."

We are told that Keach was kept a close prisoner until the following Saturday, and on that day was carried to the pillory at Aylesbury, where he stood two hours without being permitted to speak to the spectators. It is recorded that his hands as well as his head were carefully kept in the pillory the whole time. The next Thursday he stood in the same manner and length of time at Winslow, the town where he lived, and his book was burnt before him. "After this," we learn from Howell's "State Trials," "upon paying his fine, and giving sufficient security for his good behaviour, he was set at liberty ; but was never brought to make recantation."

Thomas Disney, who appears to have been a

minister at Stoke Hamond, Bucks, addressed to
Luke Wilkes a letter, as follows :

" Honoured Sir,
                   And loving Brother this Primer owned by
Benjamin Keach as the Author and bought by my man
George Chilton for five pence of Henry Keach of Stableford
Mill neare me, a miller ; who then sayd that his brother
Benjamin Keach is author of it, and that there are fiveteene
hundred of them printed.   This Benjamin Keach is a Tayler,
and one that is a teacher in this new fangled way, and lives
at Winslow, a market towne in Buckinghamshire.   Pray take
some speedie course to acquaint my Lord Archbishop his grace
with it, whereby his authoritie may issue forth that ye
impression may be seized upon before they be much more
dispersed to ye poysoining of people ; they contayning, (as I
conceive) factious, schismaticall, and hereticall matter.   Some
are scattered in my parish, and perchance in no place sooner,
because he hath a sister here and some others of his gang, two
whereof I have bought up.   Pray let me have your speedie
account of it.   I doubt not but it will be taken as acceptable
service to God's Church, and beleeve it a very thankefull
obligement to

Stoke hamond in   Honoured Sir
Bucks—64   Your truely loving Brother
May 26th   Thomas Disney.
         (Addressed)
                             These for his honoured friend Luke
                             Wilkes esqre. at Whitehall with speed
                             pray present."

The above is from the State Papers of the period.
    Defoe wrote much and well.   He was by birth
and education a Dissenter, and with much ability
asserted the rights of Nonconformists.   At a
time when Churchmen were trying to obtain hard

measures against the Dissenters, he directed against the Church party a severe satire, under the title of " The Shortest Way with the Dissenters." It exasperated the members of the Government, and a reward of fifty pounds was offered for his apprehension. The advertisement respecting him is a literary curiosity, and appeared in *The London Gazette.* It reads as follows :

" Whereas Daniel De Foe, *alias* De Fooe, is charged with writing a scandalous and seditious pamphlet, entitled, ' The Shortest Way with the Dissenters.' He is a middle-sized, spare man, about forty years old, of a brown complexion, and dark brown coloured hair, but wears a wig, a hooked nose, a sharp chin, grey eyes, and a large mole near his mouth ; was born in London, and for many years was a hose factor, in Truman's-yard, in Cornhill, and now is owner of a brick and pantile works near Tilbury-fort, in Essex. Whoever shall discover the said Daniel De Foe to any of Her Majesty's principal Secretaries of State, or any of Her Majesty's Justices of the Peace, so as he may be apprehended, shall have a reward of fifty pounds, which Her Majesty has ordered immediately to be paid upon such discovery."

Defoe managed to keep out of the way of the authorities, but on hearing that the printer and publisher of the pamphlet were put into prison, he gave himself up, and they were set at liberty. He was tried at the Old Bailey, in July, 1704, and pleaded guilty. It is said that he put in this plea on the promise of pardon secretly given to him. He did not, however, escape punishment ;

he was fined two hundred marks, ordered to appear three times in the pillory, and remain in prison during the Queen's pleasure.

During his imprisonment before being placed in the pillory, he wrote the famous " Hymn to the Pillory," which was speedily put into type and sung by the crowd at the time Defoe was in the pillory.   Here are some lines from it:

> Hail hieroglyphic State machine,
> Contrived to punish fancy in ;
> Men that are men, in thee can feel no pain,
> And all thy insignificants disdain,
> Contempt, that false new word for shame,
> Is, without crime, an empty name ;
> A shadow to amuse mankind,
> But ne'er to fright the wise or well-fixed mind.
> Virtue despises human scorn !
>   .   .   .   .
> Even learned Seldon saw
> A prospect of thee through the law.
> He had thy lofty pinnacles in view,
> But so much honour never was thy due.
>   .   .   .   .
> The first intent of laws
> Was to correct the effect, and check the cause,
> And all the ends of punishment
> Were only future mischiefs to prevent.
> But justice is interverted, when
> Those engines of the law,
> Instead of pinching vicious men,
> Keep honest ones in awe.
>   .   .   .   .
> Tell them the men that placed him there
> Are friends unto the times ;

But at a loss to find his guilt,
And can't commit his crimes.

Defoe fared well in the pillory. He was not pelted with rotten eggs, but with flowers; and beautiful garlands were suspended from the pillory. In a modest manner, he gave an account of the affair. "The people," he wrote, "were expected to treat me very ill, but it was not so. On the contrary, they were with me—wished those who had set me there were placed in my room, and expressed their affections by loud thanks and acclamations when I was taken down."

There is not the least truth in Pope's well-known, and we may say disgraceful line :

Earless, on high stood unabash'd De Foe.

After Defoe had spent about a year in prison, the Queen sent to his wife money to pay the fine.

A work was issued in 1704, entitled, "The Superiority and Dominion of the Crown of England over the Crown of Scotland," by William Attwood. The Scottish Parliament had the publication under consideration, and pronounced it scurrilous and full of falsehoods, and finally commanded the public hangman of Edinburgh to burn the book.

Williams, the bookseller, was put in the pillory in the year 1765, for republishing the *North Briton* in forty-five volumes. " The coach," says *The Gentleman's Magazine*, " that carried him from the King's Bench Prison to the pillory was No. 45. He was received with the acclamations of a prodigious concourse of people. Opposite to the pillory was erected two ladders, with cords running from each other, on which were hung a jack-boot, an axe, and a Scotch bonnet. The latter, after remaining some time, was burnt, and the top-boot chopped off. During his standing, also, a purple purse, ornamented with ribbands of an orange colour, was produced by a gentleman, who began a collection in favour of the culprit by putting a guinea into it himself, after which, the purse being carried round, many contributed, to the amount in the whole, as supposed, of about two hundred guineas."

The spectators loudly cheered Mr. Williams on getting into and out of the pillory. He held a sprig of laurel in his hand during the time he was confined in the pillory.

Alexander Wilson, the famous ornithologist and poet, in the year 1793, was tried for publishing some satirical poems concerning certain

Paisley manufacturers. The pieces were regarded as libellous, and he was fined £12 13s. 6d., and condemned to burn in a public manner his poems at the Market Cross at Paisley. The poet was unable to pay the fine, and had to go to prison for a short time. The circumstance was the chief cause of Wilson leaving Scotland for America.

A very large number of books taken from the monasteries were burned in France in the year 1790. At Paris, 808,120 volumes were consumed by fire, and in the whole country the total is said to have exceeded 4,194,412, and of this large number, 2,000,000 were on theology, and 26,000 were manuscripts.

In speaking of France, we are reminded of a story related of Voltaire, and with it we may fitly close this section. During a visit to the King of Prussia, at Berlin, he wrote on his Majesty a far from complimentary epigram. He was punished by the sergeant-at-arms for the offence, and compelled to write a receipt acknowledging that he had been flogged. It ran as follows :

"Received from the right hand of Conrad Bochoffner, thirty lashes on my bare back, being in full for an epigram on Frederick III., King of Prussia. Vive le Roi."

Finger=Pillory.

FINGER-PILLORIES, or stocks, in past
ages, were probably frequently employed in
the old manorial halls of England; but at the
present period only traces of few are to be found.
The most interesting example is one in the parish
church of Ashby-de-la-Zouch, Leicestershire,
which has been frequently described and
illustrated. An account of it appears in *Notes
and Queries* of October 25th, 1851. It is
described as "fastened at its right hand extremity
into a wall, and consists of two pieces of oak; the
bottom and fixed piece is three feet eight inches
long; the width of the whole is four-and-a-half
inches, and when closed, it is five inches deep:
the left hand extremity is supported by a leg of
the same width as the top, and two feet six
inches in length; the upper piece is joined to the
lower by a hinge, and in this lower and fixed
horizontal part are a number of holes, varying in
size; the largest are towards the right hand:

these holes are sufficiently deep to admit the
finger to the second joint, and a slight hollow is
made to admit the third one, which lies flat;
there is, of course, a corresponding hollow at the
top of the moveable part, which, when shut down,
encloses the whole finger." Thomas Wright,
F.S.A., in his " Archæological Album," gives an
illustration of the Ashby-de-la-Zouch example,

FINGER-PILLORY, ASHBY-DE-LA-ZOUCH.

and we reproduce a copy. "It shows the manner
in which the finger was confined, and it will
easily be seen that it could not be withdrawn
until the pillory was opened. If the offender
were held long in this posture, the punishment
must have been extremely painful."

Amongst the old-time relics at Littlecote Hall,
an ancient Wiltshire mansion, may still be seen

a finger-pillory. It is made of oak. We give an illustration of it from a drawing executed expressly for this work. At Littlecote Hall it is spoken of as an instrument of domestic punishment.

Plot, in his "History of Staffordshire," published in 1686, gives an illustration of one of

FINGER-PILLORY, LITTLECOTE HALL.

these old-time finger-pillories. "I cannot forget," writes Plot, "a piece of art that I found in the Hall of the Right Honourable William Lord Paget, at Beaudesart, made for the punishment of disorders that sometimes attend feasting, in Christmas time, etc., called the finger-stocks, into

which the Lord of Misrule used to put the fingers
of all such persons as committed misdemeanours,
or broke such rules, as, by consent, were agreed
on for the time of keeping Christmas among the
servants and others of promiscuous quality ; there
being divided in like manner, as the stocks of the
legs, and having holes of different sizes to fit for
scantlings of all fingers, as represented in the
table." We reproduce a sketch of Plot's picture.

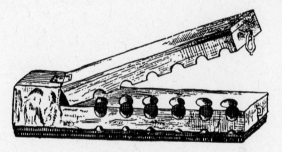

FINGER-PILLORY, BEAUDESART.

In an account of the Customs of the Manor of
Ashton-under-Lyne, in the fifteenth century, it is
stated at the manorial festivals, " in order to
preserve as much as possible the degree of decorum
that was necessary, there were frequently introduced a diminutive pair of stone stocks of about
eighteen inches in length, for confining within
them the fingers of the unruly."

The Jougs.

THIS old-time instrument of punishment was more generally used in Scotland than in England. It was employed in Holland, and most likely in other countries. In Scotland, its history may be traced back to the sixteenth century, and from that period down to about a hundred years ago, it was a popular means of enforcing ecclesiastical discipline, and it was also brought into requisition for punishing persons guilty of the lesser civil offences. In North Britain the jougs were usually fastened to a church door, a tree in a churchyard, or to the post of a church gate, a market cross, a market tron, or weighing-post, and not infrequently to prison doors.

The jougs are simple in form, consisting of an iron ring or collar, with a joint or hinge at the back to permit it being opened and closed, and in the front are loops for the affixing of a padlock to secure it round the neck of the culprit.

The "Diary of Henry Machyn, Citizen and Merchant-Taylor of London, from A.D. 1550 to A.D. 1563" (published by the Camden Society in 1848), contains the following note on the use of

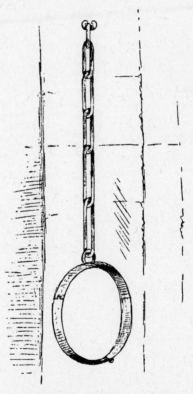

THE JOUGS, PRIORY CHURCH, BRIDLINGTON.

the jougs : "The 30th day of June, 1553," it is stated, "was set a post hard by the Standard in Cheap, and a young fellow tied to the post with a collar of iron about his neck, and another to the post with a chain, and two men with two whips whipping them about the post, for pretended visions and opprobrious and seditious words." We have modernised the spelling of Machyn.

Disregarding parental authority in Scotland was frequently the cause of young folks being punished by the jougs, and in other ways. Harsh rules of life were by no means confined to North Britain. In Tudor England manners were severe and formal, parents extracting abject deference from their offspring. A child did not presume to speak or sit down without leave in presence of its parents. A little leniency was extended to girls, for when tired they might kneel on cushions at the far end of the room; but boys were expected to stand with their heads uncovered. It is to be feared that true domestic bliss was almost unknown in olden times. Teachers were equally tyrannical, and it is a matter of history that Robert Ascham, the tutor of Queen Elizabeth, used to " pinch, nip, and bob [slap] the princess when she displeased him."

Some very curious facts relating to this subject were drawn from the old Kirk-Session records, by the Rev. Charles Rogers, LL.D., for his " Social

Life in Scotland," an important work printed for the Grampian Club. "David Leyes, who struck his father," was, says Dr. Rogers, by a Kirk-Session of St. Andrews, in 1574, sentenced to appear before the congregation "bairheddit and beirfuttit, upon the highest degree of the penitent stuool, with a hammer in the ane hand and ane stane in the uther hand, as the twa instruments he mannesit his father,—with ane papir writin in great letteris about his heid with these wordis, 'Behold the onnaturall Son, punished for putting hand on his father, and dishonouring of God in him.'" Nor was this deemed sufficient humiliation, for the offender was afterwards made to stand at the market cross two hours "in the jaggs, and thereafter cartit through the haill toun." It was also resolved that "if ever he offended father or mother heireafter, the member of his body quhairly he offendit salbe cuttit off from him, be it tung, hand or futt without mercy, as examples to utheris abstein fra the lyke." At Glasgow, in the year 1598, the Presbytery carefully considered the conduct of a youth who had passed his father "without lifting his bonnet."

A servant at Wigtown, in 1694, was brought before the magistrates for raising her hand and abusing her mistress, and was ordered to stand a full hour with the jougs round her neck.

At Rothesay, a woman gave the members of the Kirk-Session a great deal of trouble through departing from the path of sobriety. Persuasion and rebuke were tried without avail. At last, in the year 1661, the Session warned her that "if hereafter she should be found drunk, she would be put in the jouggs and have her dittay written on her face."

Mr. James S. Thomson read a paper before the Dumfries Antiquarian Society, supplying some interesting glimpses of bygone times furnished by the Kirk-Session Records of Dumfries. Not the least important information was that relating to punishments of the past. It will not be without interest to notice a few of the cases. In the year 1637, a man named Thomas Meik had been found guilty of slandering Agnes Fleming, and he was sentenced to stand for a certain time in the jougs at the tron, and subsequently on his bare knees at the market cross to ask her pardon.

The case of Bessie Black was investigated, and it was proved that for the third time she had been found guilty of leaving the path of virtue, and for her transgressions she was directed for six

Sabbaths to stand at the Cross in the jougs. In another case it was proved that two servants had been found guilty of scolding each other, and sentence was given that they were "to be put into the jougs presently." A curious sentence was passed in the year 1644. A man and his wife were ordered to stand at the Kirk-style with their hands in their mouths.

Exposure of persons to the contempt of the public was formerly a common form of punishment in Scotland. Curious information bearing on the subject may be gleaned from the old newspapers. We gather from the columns of the *Aberdeen Journal*, for the year 1759, particulars of three women, named Janet Shinney, Margaret Barrack, and Mary Duncan, who suffered by being exposed in public. "Upon trial," it is reported, "they were convicted, by their own confessions, of being in the practice, for some time past, of stealing and resetting tea and sugar, and several other kinds of merchant's goods, from a merchant in the town. And the Magistrates have sentenced them to be carried to the Market Cross of Aberdeen, on Thursday the 31st [May, 1759], at twelve o'clock at noon, and to be tied to a stake bareheaded for one hour, by the executioner, with a rope about each of their necks, and a paper on their breasts denoting their crime ; to be removed to prison, and taken down again on Friday the 1st June at twelve o'clock, and to stand an hour at the Market Cross in the manner above mentioned ; and thereafter to be transported through the whole streets of the town in a cart bareheaded (for the greater ignominy), with the executioner and tuck of drum, and to be banished the burgh and liberties in all time coming." In bygone ages, it was a common custom to banish persons from towns for frail conduct. A woman at Dumfries, for example, was for a fourth lapse from virtue sentenced " to be carted from the toun."

We have been favoured with an interesting note bearing on banishing a woman, by Mr. William Wilson of Sanquhar, a gentleman who takes a deep delight in all that relate to the " days o' langsyne." The last case of banishing a person from Sanquhar occurred some sixty years since, and there are old people still living who remember it. A fine-looking young woman had been found guilty of a petty theft, and was sentenced to be drummed out of the town. She was accordingly brought out of the gaol; round her neck was tied a rope, and the end of it was held by the jailor. A paper was pinned to her back bearing an inscription, thus, "This is a Thief." She was led the whole length of the main street and back. A man followed on her heels, beating a drum to attract the attention of the public. She was then ordered to quit the town.

At a meeting of the Kirk-Session at Lesmahago, held in June, 1697, the case of a shepherd who had shorn his sheep on the Parish Fast was seriously discussed, with a view of severely punishing him for the offence. A minute as follows was passed : "The Session, considering that there are several scandals of this nature breaking forth, recommends to the bailie of the bailerie of Lesmahago to fix a pair of jougs at the kirk door, that he may cause punish corporally those who are not able to pay fines, and that according to law."

A common word in Ayrshire for the jougs was " bregan." In the accounts of the parish of Mauchline is an entry as under :

> 1681.   For a lock to the bregan and
> mending it £1 16   0

In Jamieson's "Dictionary" it is spelled " brad-

yeane." Persons neglecting to attend church on
the Sunday were frequently put into the jougs.
Several cases of this case might be cited, but
perhaps particulars of one will be sufficient. A
man named John Persene was brought before the
Kirk-Session of Galston, in 1651. He admitted
he had not been to church for the space of five
weeks. He, for thus neglecting to attend to the
ordinances, was " injoyned to apier in the public
place of repentence, and there to be publicly
rebuked, with certificatione that if he be found to
be two Sabbaths together absent from the church
he shall be put in the breggan."

In " Prehistoric Annals of Scotland," by
Daniel Wilson, LL.D. (London, 1863), there is a
drawing of a fine old pair of jougs, " found," says
Wilson, " imbedded in a venerable ash tree,
recently blown down, at the churchyard gate,
Applegirth, Dumfriesshire. The tree, which was
of great girth, is believed to have been upwards
of three hundred years old, and the jougs were
completely imbedded in its trunk, while the chain
and staple hung down within the decayed and
hollow core." The jougs belonging to the parish
of Galashiels are preserved at Abbotsford. At
Merton, Berwickshire, the jougs may be seen

at the church. The Fenwick jougs are still fastened to the church wall, and the old Session Records of the parish contain references to cases where persons were ordered to "stand in the jougs from eight till ten, and thence go to the place of repentence within ye kirk." At the village of Kilmaurs, Ayrshire, the jougs are

JOUGS FROM THE OLD CHURCH OF COVA, FORFARSHIRE.

attached to the old Tolbooth, at the town of Kinross are fastened to the market cross, and at Sanquhar they are in front of the town hall.

We give three illustrations of the jougs. One represents a very fine example, which may be seen in the Priory Church of Bridlington, Yorkshire. We believe that this is the first picture which has been published of this interesting old-time relic. It is referred to in the local guide books, but no information is given saying when last used.

It is stated in the "History of Wakefield Cathedral," by John W. Walker, F.S.A., that "an old chain, leaded into the wall at the junction of

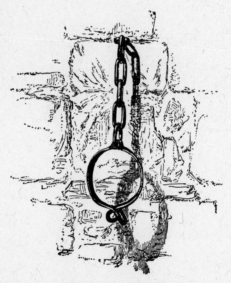

THE JOUGS, AT DUDDINGSTON.

the north aisle with the tower in the interior of the church, is said to have been used for the purpose of fastening up persons who disturbed the service." We think that it may be safely assumed that formerly the jougs were affixed at the end of the chain.

In the Museum of the Society of Antiquaries of Scotland, Edinburgh, may be seen the jougs of the old parish church of Cova, Forfarshire. This interesting museum also contains other specimens. About a mile from Edinburgh is the charming hamlet of Duddingston, and at the churchyard gate are the jougs, which form a curious link between the ruder customs of bygone ages and the more refined life of modern times.

The Stocks.

IN some of the remoter villages of England, where ancient customs linger the longest, may still be seen the remains of the old parish stocks, and in a few places the stocks themselves still stand in their original form.

Stocks were used, at an early period, as a means of punishing breakers of the law. The precise dated when they were first employed in this country is not known, but we may infer from Anglo-Saxon illustrations, that the stocks were in general use amongst

ANGLO-SAXON PUNISHMENTS.

the Anglo-Saxons, for they often figure in drawings of their public places. The picture we here give is from the Harleian MS., No. 65. The stocks were usually placed by the side of the public road, at the entrance of a town. It will be observed that two offenders are fastened to the columns of a public building by means of a rope or chain. It has been suggested, and is most likely a court-house. The "Cambridge Trinity College Psalter"—an illuminated manuscript— presents some curious illustrations of the manners of the earlier half of the twelfth century. We give a reproduction of one of its quaint pictures. Two men are in the stocks; one, it will be seen, is held by one leg only, and the other by both,

TAUNTING PERSONS IN THE STOCKS.

and a couple of persons are taunting them in their time of trouble.

Stocks were not only used as a mode of punishment, but as means of securing offenders. In bygone times, every vill of common right was compelled to erect a pair of stocks at its own expense. The constable by common law might place persons in the stocks to keep them in hold, but not by way of punishment.

We gather from an act passed during the reign
of Edward III., in the year 1351, and known as
the Second Statute of Labourers, that if artificers
were unruly they were liable to be placed in the
stocks. Some years later, namely, in 1376,

IN THE PARISH STOCKS, BY ALFRED CROWQUILL.

the Commons prayed that the stocks might be
established in every village. In 1405, an Act
was passed for every town and village to be
provided with a pair of stocks, so that a place

which had not this instrument of punishment and detention was regarded as a hamlet. Mr. S. M. Morris, in his privately-printed work on "The Obsolete Punishments of Shropshire," has an interesting note bearing on this point. "No village," says Mr. Morris, "was considered to be complete, or even worthy of the name of village, without its stocks, so essential to due order and government were they deemed to be. A Shropshire historian, speaking of a hamlet called Hulston, in the township of Middle, in order, apparently, to prove calling the place a hamlet and not a village he was speaking correctly, remarks in proof of his assertion, that Hulston did not then, or ever before, possess a constable, a pound, or stocks."

Wynkyn de Worde, who, in company with Richard Pynsent, succeeded to Caxton's printing business, in the year 1491, issued from their press the play of "Hick Scorner," and in one of the scenes the stocks are introduced. The works of Shakespeare include numerous allusions to this subject. "Thus," says Dyer, in "The Folk-Lore of Shakespeare," "Launce, in 'The Two Gentlemen of Verona' (IV. 4), says : 'I have sat in the stocks for puddings he hath stolen.' In 'All's

Well that Ends Well' (IV. 3), Bertram says :
' Come, bring forth this counterfeit module has
deceived me, like a double-meaning prophesier.'
Whereupon one of the French lords adds : ' Bring
him forth ; has sat i' stocks all night, poor gallant
knave.' Volumnia says of Coriolanus (V. 3) :

> ' There's no man in the world
> More bound to 's mother ; yet here lets me prate
> Like one i' the stocks.'

Again, in the ' Comedy of Errors' (III. 1),
Luce speaks of ' a pair of stocks in the town,'
and in ' King Lear' (II. 2), Cornwall, referring
to Kent, says :

> ' Fetch forth the stocks !
> You stubborn ancient knave.' "

It would seem that formerly, in great houses, as
in some colleges, there were movable stocks for
the correction of the servants.

In Butler's " Hudebras" are allusions to the
stocks. Says the poet :

> " An old dull sot, who toll'd the clock
> For many years at Bridewell-dock ;
>
> .   .   .   .   .   .
>
> " Engaged the constable to seize
> All those that would not break the peace ;
> Let out the stocks and whipping-post,
> And cage, to those that gave him most."

We are enabled, by the kindness of Mr. Austin Dobson, author of "Thomas Bewick and his Pupils," to reproduce from that work a picture of the stocks, engraved by Charlton Nesbit for Butler's "Hudebras," 1811.

Scottish history contains allusions to the stocks; but in North Britain they do not appear

IN THE STOCKS, BY NESBIT

to have been so generally used as in England. On the 24th August, 1623, a case occupied the attention of the members of the Kirk-Session of Kinghorn. It was proved that a man named William Allan had been guilty of abusing his wife on the Sabbath, and for the offence was condemned to be placed twenty-four hours in the stocks, and subsequently to stand in the jougs two hours on a market day. It was further intimated to him that if he again abused his wife, he would be banished from the town.

It was enacted, in the year 1605, that every person convicted of drunkenness should be fined five shillings or spend six hours in the stocks, and James I., in the year 1623, confirmed the Act. Stocks were usually employed for punishing drunkards, but drunkenness was by no means the only offence for which they were brought into requisition. We learn from the " Social History of the Southern Counties of England," by George Roberts, that wood-stealers, or, as they were styled, " hedge-tearers," were, about 1584, set in the stocks two days in the open street, with the stolen wood before them, as a punishment for a second offence. Vagrants were in former times often put in the stocks, and Canning's " Needy Knife-Grinder" was taken for one, and punished.

In a valuable work mainly dealing with Devonshire, by A. H. A. Hamilton, entitled, " Quarter Sessions from Queen Elizabeth to Queen Anne," there is an important note on this subject. " A favourite punishment," says Hamilton, " for small offences, such as resisting a constable, was the stocks. The offender had to come into the church at morning prayer, and say publicly that he was sorry, and was then set in the stocks until the end of the evening prayer. The punishment was generally repeated on the next market day."

Tippling on a Sunday during public divine service was in years agone a violation of the laws, and frequently was the means of offenders being placed in the stocks. In Sheffield, from a record dated February 12th, 1790, we find that for drinking in a public-house, during the time of service in the church, nine men were locked in the stocks. "Two boys," we find it is stated in the same work, "were made to do penance in the church for playing at trip during divine service, by standing in the midst of the church with their trip sticks erect.

Not far distant from Sheffield is the village of Whiston, and here remain the old parish stocks near to the church, and bear the date of 1786.

Perhaps the most notable person ever placed in the stocks for drinking freely, but not wisely, was Cardinal Wolsey. He was, about the year 1500, the incumbent as Lymington, near Yeovil, and at the village feast had overstepped the bounds of moderation, and his condition being made known to Sir Amias Poulett, J.P., a strict moralist, he was, by his instructions, humiliated by being placed in the stocks.   It was the general practice in bygone days, not very far remote, for church-wardens to visit the various public-houses during

WHISTON STOCKS.

the time of church service and see that no persons were drinking.   At Beverley, about 1853, the representatives of the church were on their rounds, and met in the streets a well-known local character called Jim Brigham, staggering along the street.   The poor fellow was taken into custody, and next day brought before the Mayor, and after being severely spoken to about the sin of Sunday tippling, he was sentenced to the stocks for two hours. An eye-witness to Jim's punishment says : "While he was in the stocks, one of the Corporation officials placed in Jim's hat a sheet of paper, stating the cause of his punishment and its extent. A young man who had been articled to a lawyer, but who was not practising, stepped forward, and taking the paper out, tore it into shreds, remarking it was no part of Jim's sentence to be subjected to that additional disgrace. The act was applauded by the on-lookers. One working-man, who sympathised with him, filled and lit a tobacco pipe, and placed it in Jim's mouth ; but it was instantly removed by one of the constables, who considered it was a most flagrant act, and one calling for prompt interference on the part of the guardians of the law." Brigham was the last person punished in the stocks at Beverley. The stocks, which bear the date 1789, were movable, and fitted into sockets near the Market Cross. They are still preserved in a chamber at St. Mary's in that town. The Minster had also its stocks, which are still preserved in the roof of that splendid edifice.

The stocks were last used at Market Drayton some fifty years ago. " It is related," writes Mr. Morris, "that some men, for imbibing too freely and speaking unseemly language to parishioners, as they were going to church on a Sunday morning, were, on the following day, duly charged with the offence and fined, the alternative being confinement for four hours in the stocks. Two of the men refused to pay the fine, and were consequently put therein. The people flocked around them, and, while some regaled them with an ample supply of beer, others expressed their sympathy in a more practical way by giving them money, so that, when released, their heads and their pockets were considerably heavier than they had been on the previous Sunday." At Ellesmere, the stocks, whipping-post, and pillory were a combination of engines of punishment. The former were frequently in use for the correction of drunkards. A regular customer, we read, was " honoured by a local poet with some impromptu verses not unworthy of reproduction :

> 'A tailor here ! confined in stocks,
>   A prison made of wood—a—,
> Weeping and wailing to get out,
>   But couldna' for his blood—a—

The pillory, it hung o'er his head,
The whipping-post so near—a—
A crowd of people round about
Did at William laugh and jeer—a—'"

" The style was," it is said, " a sarcastic imitation
of ' William's ' peculiar manner of speaking when
tipsy."

Mr. Christopher A. Markham has collected
much out-of-the-way information on the history
of ancient punishments, and included many items
of more than local interest in a paper he read at a
meeting of a learned society in 1886. In his
notices of Gretton stocks, he says they " still
stand on the village green ; they were made to
secure three men, and have shackles on the post
for whipping ; they are in a good state of repair.
Joshua Pollard, of Gretton, was placed in them,
in the year 1857, for six hours, in default of paying
five shillings and cost for drunkenness." In the
following year a man was put in the stocks
for a similar offence. It is asserted that a man
was placed in the Aynhoe stocks in 1846 for
using bad language. Card-sharpers and the like
often suffered in the stocks. It appears from
the *Shrewsbury Chronicle* of May 1st, 1829, that
the punishment in the stocks was inflicted " at

Shrewsbury on three Birmingham youths for imposing on 'the flats' of the town with the games of 'thimble and pea' and 'prick the garter.'" A very late instance of a man being placed in the stocks for gambling was recorded in a Leeds newspaper, under date of April 14th, 1860. "A notorious character," it is stated, "named John Gambles, of Stanningley, having been convicted some months ago for Sunday gambling, and sentenced to sit in the stocks for six hours, left the locality, returned lately, and suffered his punishment by sitting in the stocks from two till eight o'clock on Tuesday last." Several writers on this old form of punishment regard the foregoing as the latest instance of a person being confined in the stocks; it is, however, not the case, for one Mark Tuck at Newbury, Berkshire, in 1872, was placed in them. The following particulars are furnished in *Notes and Queries*, 4th series, vol. x., p. 6: "A novel scene was presented in the Butter and Poultry Market, at Newbury, on Tuesday (June 11th, 1872) afternoon. Mark Tuck, a rag and bone dealer, who for several years had been well known in the town as a man of intemperate habits, and upon whom imprisonment in Reading gaol had failed to produce any beneficial effect, was fixed in the stocks for drunkenness and disorderly conduct in the Parish Church on Monday evening. Twenty-six years had elapsed since the stocks were last used, and their reappearance created no little sensation and amusement, several hundreds of persons being attracted to the spot where they were fixed. Tuck was seated upon a stool, and his legs were secured in the stocks at a few minutes past one o'clock, and as the church clock, immediately facing him, chimed each quarter, he uttered expressions of thankfulness, and seemed anything but pleased at the laughter and derision of the crowd. Four hours having passed, Tuck was released, and by a little stratagem on the part of the police, he escaped without being interfered with by the crowd."

STOKESLEY STOCKS
AND
WHIPPING-POST.

Mr. George Markham Tweddell, the historian of Cleveland, informs us that the Stokesley stocks were used about forty years ago. The public were so disgusted with the disorder which wsa caused, that this antiquated practice was never renewed, much to the chagrin of the two

constables, who had hoped to revive the ancient
punishment, for which purpose the old stocks had
been newly repaired.

Attendance and repairing stocks formed quite
important items in old parish accounts. A few
entries drawn from the township account-
books of Skipton may be reproduced as examples:

	s.	d.
April 16th, 1763.—For taking up a man and setting in ye stocks	2	0
March 27th, 1739.—For mending stocks—wood and iron work...	9	6
July 12th, 1756.—For pillory and stocks renewing	3	6
March 25th, 1776.—Paid John Lambert for repairing the stocks...	5	6
March 25th, 1776.—Paid Christ. Brown for repairing the stocks	4	6

The foregoing entries are reproduced from the
"History of Skipton," by Mr. W. H. Dawson. He
says "during their later years, the stocks were used
almost solely on Sundays." A practice prevailed
at Skipton similar to the one we have described
at Beverley. "At a certain stage in the morning
service at the church," writes Mr. Dawson, "the
churchwardens of the town and country parishes
withdrew, and headed by the old beadle walked
through the streets of the town. If a person was
found drunk in the streets, or even drinking in
one of the inns, he was promptly escorted to the

stocks, and impounded for the remainder of the morning. An imposing personage was the beadle. He wore a cocked hat, trimmed, as was his official coat, with gold, and he carried about with him in majestic style a trident staff. 'A terror to evil-doers' he certainly was—at anyrate, to those of tender years." The churchwardens not infrequently partook of a slight refreshment during their Sunday morning rounds, and we remember seeing in the police reports of a Yorkshire town that some highly respectable representatives of the church had been fined for drinking at an inn during their tour of inspection.

Not a few men think that the stocks might be again used with advantage. A poetical friend, Mr. John Cotton, of Birmingham, writes as follows:

"Thus, times and customs, men and manners change,
    And so all institutions have their day;
Like instruments of torture, out of range
    Of memory, the stocks will pass away,
    And with them those that 'neath yon tree decay.

The ducking-stool is done with, and the helm,
    Contrivances ordained for scolding wives;
The pillory is banished from the realm,
    And corporal punishment no longer thrives,
    Save through the cat, which now alone survives.

Each mode has served its turn, and played a part
    For good or ill with man; but while the bane

Of drunkenness corrupts the nation's heart—
Discrediting our age—methinks the reign
Of stocks, at least, were well revived again."

" At Bramhall, Cheshire," says Mr. Alfred
Burton, to whom we are indebted for several
illustrations and many valuable notes in this book,
" the stocks were perfect till 1887, when the leg-
stones were unfortunately taken away, and cannot
now be found. Thomas Leah, about 1849, was

STOCKS AT BRAMHALL.

the last person put into them. He went to the
constable and asked to be placed in the stocks, a
request that was granted, and he remained there
all night. On the 9th August, 1822, two women
were incarcerated in the stocks in the market
place at Stockport, for three hours, one for getting
drunk, the other for gross and deliberate scandal.

The editor of the *New York Herald* pays much
attention to old-world lore, and in his columns

much that is curious and entertaining finds a place.
On the 29th of June, 1890, a paper was devoted
to a pretty bit of old English scenery, entitled,
"Under the Chilterns." Aldbury is described
thus : " In the centre of the village green stands a
huge elm, its gnarled roots worn into caverns or
recesses. By it stands the stocks, and close to
these a placid pool, on whose mossy margin a

STOCKS AT ALDBURY.

dozen swallows are busy with ceaseless fluttering
of purple-black wings and snowy breasts."

In closing this chapter we must not omit to
state that in the olden time persons refusing to
assist in getting in the corn or hay harvest were
liable to be imprisoned in the stocks. At the
Northamptonshire Quarter Sessions held in 1688,
the time was fixed at two days and one night.

The Drunkard's Cloak.

SEVERAL historians, dealing with the social
life of England in bygone times, have
described the wearing of a barrel after the manner
of a cloak as a general mode of punishing
drunkards, in force during the Commonwealth.
There appears to be little foundation for the
statement, and, after careful consideration, we
have come to the conclusion that this mode
of punishment was, as regards this country,
confined to Newcastle-on-Tyne.

In the year 1655 was printed in London a
work entitled, "England's Grievance Discovered
in Relation to the Coal Trade," by Ralph
Gardner, of Chirton, in the county of Northumberland, Gent. The book is dedicated to
"Oliver, Lord Protector." Gardner not only
gave a list of grievances, but suggested measures
to reform them. It will be gathered from the
following proposed remedy that he was not any
advocate of half measures in punishing persons

guilty of offences. He suggested that a law be created for death to such that shall commit perjury, forgery, or accept bribery.

More than one writer has said that Gardner was executed in 1661, at York, for coining, but there is not any truth in the statement. We have proof that he was conducting his business after the year it is stated that he suffered death at the hands of the public executioner.

Gardner, in his work, gave depositions of witnesses to support his charges against "the tyrannical oppression of the magistrates of New-castle-on-Tyne." "John Willis, of Ipswich," he writes, "upon his oath said, that he, and this deponent, was in Newcastle six months ago, and there he saw one Ann Bridlestone drove through the streets by an officer of the same corporation, holding a rope in his hand, the other end fastened to an engine called the branks, which is like a crown, it being of iron, which was musled over the head and face, with a great gag or tongue of iron forced into her mouth, which forced the blood out ; and that is the punishments which the magistrates do inflict upon chiding and scoulding women ; and he hath often seen the like done to others."

" He, this deponent, further affirms, that he
hath seen men drove up and down the streets,
with a great tub or barrel opened in the sides,
with a hole in one end to put through their heads,
and so cover their shoulders and bodies, down to
the small of their legs, and then close the same,
called the new-fashioned cloak, and so make them

BRANK AND DRUNKARD'S CLOAK AT NEWCASTLE-ON-TYNE.

march to the view of all beholders; and this is
their punishments for drunkards and the like."

Several other forms of punishment are
mentioned by Gardner. Drunkards, we gather,
for the first offence were fined five shillings, to be
given to the poor, or in default of payment within
a week, were set in the stocks for six hours. For

the second offence they had to be bound for good behaviour. Scolds had to be ducked over head and ears in a ducking-stool.

" I was certainly informed," wrote Gardner, " by persons of worth, that the punishments above are but gentle admonitions to what they knew was acted by two magistrates of Newcastle : one for killing a poor workman of his own, and being questioned for it, and condemned, compounded with King James for it, paying to a Scotch lord his weight in gold and silver, every seven years or thereabouts, etc. The other magistrate found a poor man cutting a few horse sticks in his wood, for which offence he bound him to a tree, and whipt him to death."

The Rev. John Brand, in 1789, published his " History of Newcastle-on-Tyne," and reproduced in it Gardner's notice of the drunkard's cloak. Brand gives a picture of the cloak, and the Rev. J. R. Boyle, F.S.A., a leading authority on North Country bibliography, tells us that he believes it to be the first pictorial representation of the cloak. Our illustration is from Richardson's " Local Historian's Table Book." Mr. Walter Scott, publisher, of Newcastle-on-Tyne, has kindly lent us the block.

Dr. T. N. Brushfield, to whom we are under an obligation for several of the facts included in this chapter, read before the British Archæological Association, February 15th, 1888, a paper on this theme. "It is rather remarkable," said Dr. Brushfield, "that no allusion to this punishment is to be found in the Newcastle Corporation accounts or other local documents." We have reproduced from Gardner's volume the only testimony we possess of the administration of the punishment in England. There are many traces of this kind of cloak on the Continent. It is noticed in "Travels in Holland," by Sir William Brereton, under date of May 29th, 1634, as seen at Delft. John Evelyn visited Delft, on August 17th, 1641, and writes that in the Senate House "hangs a weighty vessel of wood, not unlike a butter-churn, which the adventurous woman that hath two husbands at one time is to wear on her shoulders, her head peeping out at the top only, and so led about the town, as a penance for her incontinence." Samuel Pepys has an entry in his diary respecting seeing a similar barrel at the Hague, in the year 1660. We have traces of this mode of punishment in Germany. John Howard, in his work, entitled "The State of Prisons in

England and Wales," 1784, thus writes : " Den-
mark.—Some (criminals) of the lower sort, as
watchmen, coachmen, etc., are punished by being
led through the city in what is called ' The
Spanish Mantle.' This is a kind of heavy vest,
something like a tub, with an aperture for the
head, and irons to enclose the neck. I measured
one at Berlin, 1ft. 8in. in diameter at the top, 2ft.
11in. at the bottom, and 2ft. 11in. high. . . .
This mode of punishment is particularly dreaded,
and is one cause that night robberies are never
heard of in Copenhagen."

We may safely conclude that the drunkard's
cloak was introduced into Newcastle from the
Continent. The author of a paper published in
1862, under the title of " A Look at the Federal
Army," after speaking of crossing the Susquehara,
has some remarks about punishments. " I was,"
says the writer, " extremely amused to see a
' rare ' specimen of Yankee invention, in the shape
of an original method of punishment drill. One
wretched delinquent was gratuitously framed in
oak, his head being thrust through a hole cut in
one end of a barrel, the other end of which had
been removed ; and the poor fellow ' loafed '
about in the most disconsolate manner, looking for

all the world like a half-hatched chicken. Another defaulter had heavy weights fastened to his wrists, his hands and feet being chained together." In conclusion, we are told that the punishments were as various as the crimes, but the man in the pillory-like barrel was deemed the most ludicrous.

PUNISHMENT OF A DRUNKARD.

The early English settlers in America introduced many English customs into the country. The pillory, stocks, ducking-stool, etc., were frequently employed. Drunkards were punished in various ways ; sometimes they had to wear a

large " D " in red, which was painted on a board
or card, and suspended by a string round the
neck.

At Haddon, Derbyshire, is a curious relic of
bygone times, consisting of an iron handcuff or
ring, fastened to some woodwork in the banqueting hall. If a person refused to drink the liquor
assigned to him, or committed an offence against
the convivial customs at the festive gatherings for
which this ancient mansion was so famous, his
wrist was locked in an upright position in the iron
ring, and the liquor he had declined, or a quantity
of cold water, was poured down the sleeve of his
doublet.

Whipping.

THE Anglo-Saxons whipped prisoners with a whip of three cords, knotted at the end. It was not an uncommon practice for mistresses to whip, or have their servants whipped, to death. William of Malmesbury relates a story to the effect that when King Ethelred was a child, he on one occasion displeased his mother, and she, not having a whip at hand, flogged him with some candles until he was nearly insensible with pain. " On this account," so runs the story, " he dreaded candles during the rest of his life to such a degree that he would never suffer the light of them to be introduced in his presence." During the Saxon epoch, flogging was generally adopted as a means of punishing persons guilty of offences, whether slight or serious.

For a long time in our history, payments for using the lash formed important items in the municipal accounts of towns or parish accounts of villages.

Before the monasteries were dissolved, the poor were relieved at them. No sooner had they passed away than the vagrants became a nuisance, and steps were taken to put a stop to begging; indeed, prior to this period attempts had been made to check wandering vagrants. They were referred to in the " Statute of Labourers," passed in the year 1349. Not a few enactments were made to keep down vagrancy. In the reign of Edward VI., in 1547, an Act was passed, from which it appears " that any person who had offered them work which they refused, was authorised to brand them on the breast with a V, hold them in slavery for two years, feed them during that period on bread and water, and hire them out to others." The Act failed on account of its severity, and was repealed in 1549.

It was in the reign of Henry VIII., and in the year 1530, that the famous Whipping Act was passed, directing that vagrants were to be carried to some market town or other place, " and there tied to the end of a cart naked, and beaten with whips throughout such market town, or other place, till the body shall be bloody by reason of such whipping." Vagrants, after being whipped, had to take an oath that they would return to

their native places, or where they had last dwelt
for three years. Various temporary modifications
were made to this Act, but it remained in force
until the thirty-ninth year of the reign of Queen
Elizabeth, when some important alterations were
made. Persons were not to be publicly whipped
naked, as previously, but from the middle upwards,
and whipped until the body should be bloody. It
was at this time that the whipping-post was
substituted for the cart. Whipping-posts soon
became plentiful. John Taylor, "the water
poet," in one of his works, published in 1630,
adverts to them as follows :

"In London, and within a mile, I ween,
    There are jails or prisons full eighteen,
    And sixty whipping-posts and stocks and cages."

Some of the authorities regarded with greater
favour the punishment at the whipping-post than
at the cart tail. An old writer deals at some
length with the benefit of the former. Says he :
" If to put in execution the laws of the land be of
any service to the nation, which few, I think, will
deny, the benefits of the whipping-post must be
very apparent, as being a necessary instrument to
such an execution. Indeed, the service it does to

a country is inconceivable. I, myself, know a man, who had proceeded to lay his hand upon a silver spoon with a design to make it his own, but on looking round, and seeing the whipping-post in his way, he desisted from the theft. Whether he suspected that the post would impeach him or not, I will not pretend to determine ; some folks were of opinion that he was afraid of *habeas corpus.* It is likewise an infallible remedy for all lewd and disorderly behaviour, which the chairman at sessions generally employs to restrain ; nor is it less beneficial to the honest part of mankind than the dishonest, for though it lies immediately in the high road to the gallows, it has stopped many an adventurous young man in his progress thither." The records of the Worcester Corporation contain many references to old-time punishments. In the year 1656 was made in the bye-law book a note of the fact that for some years past a want had been felt " for certain instruments for applying to the execution of justice upon offenders, namely, the pillorie, whipping-post, and gum-stoole." The Chamberlain was directed to obtain the same. We gather from the proceedings of the Doncaster Town Council that on the 5th of May, 1713, an order was made for the erection of a whipping-post, to be set up at the Stocks, Butcher-Cross, for punishing vagrants and sturdy beggars.

Notices of whipping sometimes appear in old church books. At Kingston-on-Thames, under date of September 8th, 1572, it is recorded in the parish register as follows : " This day, in this towne, was kept the sessions of Gayle Delyverye, and ther was hanged vj. persons, and xvj, taken for roges and vagabonds, and whypped abowte the market-place and brent in the ears."

At the Quarter Sessions in Devonshire, held at Easter, 1598, it was ordered that the mothers of illegitimate children be whipped. The reputed fathers had to undergo a like punishment. A very strange order was made in the same county during the Commonwealth, and it was to the effect that every woman who had been the mother of an illegitimate child, and had not been previously punished, be committed for trial. Mr. Hamilton, in his work on " The Quarter Sessions from Queen Elizabeth to Queen Anne," has many curious notes on this subject. The Scotch pedlars and others, who wended their way to push their trade in the West of England, ran a great risk of being whipped. At the Midsummer Sessions, in the year 1684, information was given to the court shewing that certain Scotch pedlars, or other petty chapmen, were in the habit of selling their goods to the "greate damage and hindrance of shopp keepers." The Court passed measures for the protection of the local tradesmen, and directed the petty constables to apprehend the strangers, and without further ceremony to strip them naked, and whip them or cause them to be openly flogged, and sent away.

The churchwardens' account of Barnsley contains references to the practice of whipping. Charges as follow occur :

1622.   William Roggers, for goinge with six wanderers
           to Ardsley ... ...   ijd.
        Mr. Garnett, for makinge them a pass ... ...   iiijd.
        Ridhard White, for whippeinge them accordinge
           to law ... ...   ijd.

The constable's accounts of the same town, from 1632 to 1636, include items similar to the following :

   To Edward Wood, for whiping of three wanderers
     sent to their dwelling-place by Sir George Plint
     and Mr. Rockley... ... ...   iiijd.

It appears from the Corporation accounts of Congleton, Cheshire, that persons were whipped at the cart tail.   We find it stated :

1637.   paid to boy for whippinge John ffoxe ... 0   2   0
         paid for a carte to tye the said ffoxe unto
             when he was whipped   0   2   0

We have told at length in the pages of " Yorkshire in Olden Times " (London : Simpkin,
Marshall & Co., 1890), the strange story of
" James Nayler, the Mad Quaker, who claimed
to be Messiah." He was examined before
Parliament in 1656, for blasphemy, and the trial
and debate lasted many hours, and the members
finally resolved " that James Nayler was guilty of
horrid blasphemy, and that he was a grand
imposter and seducer of the people," and his
sentence was, " that he should be set on the
pillory, in the Palace Yard, Westminster, during
the space of two hours, on Thursday next, and
be whipped by the hangman through the streets
from Westminster to the Old Exchange, London;
and there, likewise, he should be set on the
pillory, with his head in the pillory, for the space
of two hours, between the hours of eleven and
one, on Saturday next, in each place wearing a
paper containing an inscription of his crimes; and
that, at the Old Exchange, his tongue should be
bored through with a hot iron, and that he
should be there also stigmatised in the forehead

with the letter B ; and that he should afterwards
be sent to Bristol, to be conveyed into and

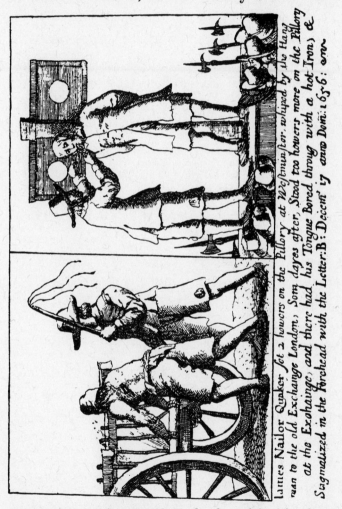

James Nailor Quaker Set 2 howers on the Pillory at Westminster. whiped by the Hand
man to the old Exchange London, Som dayes after, Stood too howers more on the Pillory
at the Exchainge, and there had his Tongue Bored throug with a hot Iron, &
Stigmatized in the Forehead with the Letter. B: Decem̄. 17 anno Dom̄i. 1656:

through the city on horseback, with his face
backwards, and there also should be whipped the

next market-day after he came thither ; and that
thence he should be committed to prison in
Bridewell, London, and there be restrained from
the society of all people, and there to labour hard
till he should be released by Parliament; and
during that time he should be debarred the use of
pen, ink, and paper, and he should have no relief
but what he earned by his daily labour." This
terrible sentence was duly carried out, although
Parliament and Cromwell were petitioned to
mitigate the punishment. During his imprisonment, he wrote his recantation in letters addressed
to the Quakers. After being confined for two
years he was set at liberty, and repaired to
Bristol, and at a public meeting made a confession
of his offence and fall. His address moved nearly
all present to tears. The Quakers once more
received him back to their Society. We reproduce an illustration from a rare picture in
possession of Dr. Brushfield, of Nayler in the
pillory, and also being whipped at the cart's
tail.

The notorious Judge Jeffreys, who, on one
occasion, in sentencing a woman to be whipped,
said : " Hangman, I charge you to pay particular
attention to this lady. Scourge her soundly,

man ; scourge her till her blood runs down ! It is Christmas, a cold time for madam to strip. See that you warm her shoulders thoroughly ! "

At Worcester, in 1697, a new whipping-post was erected in the Corn Market, at a cost of 8s. " Men and women," says a local historian, " were whipped here promiscuously in public till the close of the last century, if not later. Fourpence was the old charge for whipping male and female rogues."

The next note on whipping is drawn from the church register of Burnham, Bucks, and is one of several similar entries : " Benjamin Smat, and his wife and three children, vagrant beggars ; he of middle stature, but one eye, was this 28th day of September, 1699, with his wife and children, openly whipped at Boveney, in the parish of Burnham, in the county of Buck. according to ye laws. And they are assigned to pass forthwith from parish to parish by ye officers thereof the next direct way to the parish of St. [Se]pulchers, Lond., where they say they last inhabited three years. And they are limitted to be at St. [Se] pulch within ten days next ensuing. Given under our hands and seals, Will. Glover, Vicar of Burnham, and John Hunt, Constable of Boveney." In some instances we gather from the entries in the parish registers, after punishing the vagrants in their own parish, the authorities recommended them to the tender mercy of other persons in whose hands they might fall.

At Durham, in the year 1690, a married woman named Eleanor Wilson, was publicly whipped in the market-place, between the hours of eleven and twelve o'clock, for being drunk on Sunday, April 20th.

Insane persons did not escape the lash. In the constable's accounts of Great Staughtan, Huntingdonshire, is an item :

1690-1.   Pd. in charges taking up a distracted woman, watching her, and whipping her next day 0 8 6

A still more remarkable charge is the following in the same accounts :

1710-1.   Pd. Thomas Hawkins for whipping 2 people yt had small-pox... ... ... 0 0 8

In 1764, we gather from the *Public Ledger* that a woman, who is described as "an old offender," was conveyed in a cart from Clerkenwell Bridewell to Enfield, and publicly whipped at the cart's tail by the common hangman, for cutting down and destroying wood in Enfield

Chase. She had to undergo the punishment three times.

Persons obtaining goods under false pretences were frequently flogged. In 1769, at Nottingham, a young woman, aged nineteen, was found guilty of this crime, and was, by order of the Court of Quarter Sessions, stripped to the waist and publicly whipped on market-day in the market-place. In the following year, a female, found guilty of stealing a handkerchief from a draper's shop, was tied to the tail of a cart and whipped from Weekday-Cross to the Malt-Cross. It was at Nottingham, a few years prior to this time, that a soldier was severely punished for drinking the Pretender's health. The particulars are briefly told as follows in *Adams's Weekly Courant* for Wednesday, 20th, to Wednesday, July 27th, 1737 : "Friday last, a dragoon, belonging to Lord Cadogan's Regiment, at Nottingham, received 300 lashes, and was to receive 300 more at Derby, and to be drum'd out of the Regiment with halter about his neck, for drinking the Pretender's health."

Whipping at Wakefield appears to have been a common punishment. Payments like the following frequently occur in the constable's accounts :

1787, May 15, Assistance	at	Whiping	3 men...	0	3	0
July 6,	„	„	3 „ ...	0	3	0
Aug. 17,	„	„	2 „ ...	0	2	0
Sept. 7,	„	„	3 „ ...	0	3	0

A fire occurred at Olney in 1783, and during the confusion a man stole some ironwork. The crime was detected, and the man was tried and sentenced to be whipped at the cart's tail. Cowper, the poet, was an eye-witness to the carrying out of the sentence, and in a letter to the Rev. John Newton gives an amusing account of it. " The fellow," wrote Cowper, " seemed to show great fortitude; but it was all an imposition. The beadle who whipped him had his left hand filled with red ochre, through which, after every stroke, he drew the lash of the whip, leaving the appearance of a wound upon the skin, but in reality not hurting him at all. This being perceived by the constable, who followed the beadle to see that he did his duty, he (the constable) applied the cane, without any such management or precaution, to the shoulders of the beadle. The scene now became interesting and exciting. The beadle could by no means be induced to strike the thief hard, which provoked the constable to strike harder ; and so the double flogging continued, until a lass of Silver End, pitying the pityful beadle, thus suffering under the hands of the pityless constable, joined the procession, and placing herself immediately behind the constable, seized him by his capillary club, and pulling him backwards by the same, slapped his face with Amazonian fury. This concentration of events has taken up more of my paper than I intended, but I could not forbear to inform you how the beadle thrashed the thief, the constable the beadle, and the lady the constable, and how the thief was the only person who suffered nothing." It will be gathered from the foregoing letter that the severity of the whipping depended greatly on the caprice of the man who administered it.

A statute, in 1791, expressly forbade the whipping of female vagrants. This was certainly a much needed reform.

Persons still living remember seeing people publicly whipped in the streets. Mr. Samuel Corter Hall, born in the year 1800, in his interesting " Retrospect of a Long Life " (1883), relates that more than once he saw the cruel punishment inflicted. On the 8th of May, 1822, a man was whipped through the streets of Glasgow by the hangman for taking part in a riot.

He was the last person to undergo public whipping at the cart's tail in Glasgow.

The Rev. Wm. Cooper, B.A., the historian of the Rod, found in an old magazine a romantic story, which is well worth reproducing. " A young man who," it is stated, " was sentenced for some slight misdemeanor, to be whipped through the streets of Glasgow, proved on being stripped to be a female! She was identified at the time, by a mark on her shoulder, to be the daughter of a highly respectable merchant, who had run away from her home at an early age, and had been lost sight of for a great many years. After leaving home, she made her way to Port-Glasgow, and became cabin-boy on a West Indian sugar vessel. As her uncle was a town councillor at the time, she was pardoned the public exposure by the Lord Provost of the period, on condition of submitting to be whipped by the matron of the gaol." In the last century, it was not by any means an uncommon practice for women to run away from home in the disguise of men, and join the army or navy.

A fine example of the whipping-post still remains at Coleshill, and forms part of a pillory or stocks. It is, we believe, the only one that is left in England, although for an extended period the whipping-post was to be seen in almost every town and village of the land.

It was formerly the custom in London and other places, at the time of executions, for parents to whip their children, so as to impress upon their minds the awful lessons of the gallows. Executions were very often occurring, for people were hanged for trifling offences. Down to the year 1808, the crime for stealing from the person above the value of a shilling was punishable with death. Children must have had a hard time of it, and been frequently flogged.

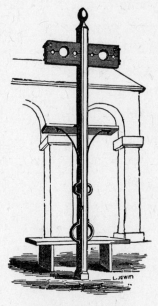

WHIPPING-POST, COLESHILL.

Whipping servants was a common practice in the olden time. Pepys and other old writers make note of it. The well-known "Diary of a Lady of Quality" contains some interesting glimpses of olden days and ways. Under date of

January 30th, 1760, Lady Francis Pennoyer, of Bullingham Court, Herefordshire, refers to one of her maids speaking in the housekeeper's room about a matter that was not to the credit of the family. My lady felt that there was truth in what the girl said, but it was not in her place to speak, and her ladyship resolved to make her know and keep her place. " She hath a pretty face," says the diarist, " and should not be too ready to speak ill of those above her in station. I should be very sorry to turn her adrift upon the world, and she hath but a poor home. Sent for her to my room, and gave her choice, either to be well whipped, or to leave the house instantly. She chose wisely, I think, and, with many tears, said I might do what I liked. I bade her attend my chamber to-morrow at twelve." Next day her ladyship writes in her diary : " Dearlove, my maid, came to my room, as I bade her. I bade her fetch the rod from what was my mother-in-law's rod-closet, and kneel and ask pardon, which she did with tears. I made her prepare, and I whipped her well. The girl's flesh is plump and firm, and she is a cleanly person—such a one, not excepting my own daughters, who are thin, and one of them, Charlotte, rather sallow, as I have

not whipped for a long time. She hath never
been whipped before, she says, since she was a
child (what can her mother and late lady have
been about, I wonder?), and she cried out a
great deal." Children and servants appear to
have been frequently flogged at Bullingham
Court, both by its lord and lady. In other
homes similar practices prevailed.

"The Tutors Assistant"

(BY GEORGE CRUIKSHANK.)

Public Penance.

CHURCH discipline in the olden days has caused the highest and lowest in the land to perform penance in public. A notable instance of a king subjecting himself to this humiliating form of punishment is that of Henry II. The story of the King's quarrels with Becket, and of his unfortunate expression which lead four knights to enact a tragic deed in Canterbury Cathedral, is familiar to the reader of history. After the foul murder of Becket had been committed, the King was in great distress, and resolved to do penance at the grave of the murdered Archbishop. Mounted on his horse, he rode for Canterbury, and on coming in sight of the Cathedral, he dismounted, and walked barefooted to Becket's shrine. He spent the day in prayer and fasting, and at night watched the relics of the saint. He next, in presence of the monks, disrobed himself, and presented his bare shoulders for them to lash.

At Canossa, in the winter of 1077, was performed a most degrading act of penance, by

Emperor Henry IV. of Germany. He had been excommunicated by Pope Gregory VII., and had suffered much on that account. He resolved to see the Pope, and, if possible, obtain absolution. The Emperor made a long and toilsome journey in the cold, in company with his loving wife, Bertha, his infant son, and only one knight. The Pope refused to see the Emperor until he had humbled himself at the gates of the castle. " On a dreary winter morning," say Baring-Gould and Gilman, in their "History of Germany," "with the ground deep in snow, the King, the heir of a line of emperors, was forced to lay aside every mark of royalty, was clad in the thin white dress of the penitent, and there fasting, he awaited the pleasure of the Pope in the castle yard. But the gates did not unclose. A second day he stood, cold, hungry, and mocked by vain hope." On the close of the third day, we are told that he was received and pardoned by the Pope.

The romantic story of Eleanor Cobham, first mistress and afterwards wife of Humphrey, Duke of Gloucester, is one of considerable interest in illustrating the strange beliefs of the olden times. The Duchess was tried in the year 1441, for treason and witchcraft. It transpired that two of her accomplices had made, by her direction, a waxen image of the reigning monarch, Henry VI. They had placed before it a slow fire, believing that the King's life would waste away as the figure. In the event of Henry's death, the Duke of Gloucester, as the nearest heir to the house of Lancaster, would have been crowned king. On the 9th November, sentence was pronounced upon the Duchess : it was to the effect that she perform public penance in three open places in London, and end her days in prison in the Isle of Man. The manner of her doing penance was as follows : " On Monday, the 13th, she came by water from Westminster, and landing at Temple Bridge, walked at noon-day through Fleet Street, bearing a waxen taper of two pounds weight, to St. Paul's, where she offered it at the high altar. On the Wednesday following, she landed at the Old Swan, and passed through Bridge Street, Gracechurch Street, and to Leadenhall, and at Cree Church, near Aldgate, made her second offering. On the ensuing Friday, she was put on shore at Queenhithe, whence she proceeded to St. Michael's Church, Cornhill, and so completed her penance. In each of these processions her head was covered only by a kerchief ; her feet were bare; scrolls, containing a narrative of her crime, were affixed to her white dress; and she was received and attended by the Mayor, Sheriff, and Companies of London."

The historian, biographer, poet, playwright, and story-teller have all related details of the career of Jane Shore. A sad tale it is, but one which has always been popular both with gentle and simple. It is not necessary to relate here at length the story of her life. She was born in London, was a woman of considerable personal charms, and could do what few ladies of her time were able to accomplish—namely, read well and write. When some sixteen or seventeen years of age, she married William Shore, a goldsmith and banker, of Lombard Street. She lived with her husband seven years, but about 1470, left him, to become one of the mistresses of Edward IV. Her beauty, wit, and pleasant behaviour rendered her popular at Court. The King died in 1483, and within two months she was charged by Richard III. with sorcery and witchcraft, but the charges could not be sustained. Her property, equal to about £20,000 at the present time, was taken from her by the King. He afterwards caused her to be brought before the Ecclesiastical Courts and tried for incontinence, and for the crime had to do penance in the streets of London. Perhaps we cannot do better than quote Rowe's poetry to relate this part of her story :

> Submissive, sad, and lonely was her look ;
> A burning taper in her hand she bore ;
> And on her shoulders, carelessly confused,
> With loose neglect her lovely tresses hung ;
> Upon her cheek a faintish flush was spread ;
> Feeble she seemed, and sorely smit with pain ;
> While, barefoot as she trod the flinty pavement,
> Her footsteps all along were marked with blood.
> Yet silent still she passed, and unrepining ;
> Her streaming eyes bent ever on the earth,
> Except when, in some bitter pang of sorrow,
> To heaven she seemed, in fervent zeal to raise,
> And beg that mercy man denied her here.

We need not go into details respecting her life from this time, but briefly state that it is a popular error to suppose that she was starved in a ditch, and that the circumstance gave rise to the name of a part of London known as Shoreditch. The black-letter ballad in the Pepys collection, which makes Jane Shore die of hunger after doing penance, and a man suffer death on the gallows for giving her bread, is without foundation. She died about 1533 or 1534, and when she was upwards of eighty years of age. It is asserted that she strewed flowers at the funeral of Henry VII.

A curious act of penance was performed in Hull, in the year 1534, by the Vicar of North Cave. He appears to have made a study of the works of the Reformers who had settled in Antwerp, and sent over their books to England. In a sermon preached in the Holy Trinity Church, Hull, he advocated their teaching, and for this he was tried for heresy and convicted. He recanted, and as an act of penance, one Sunday walked round the church barefooted, with only his shirt on, and carrying a large faggot in his hand to represent the punishment he deserved. On the next market-day, in a similar manner, he walked round the market-place of the town.

In the year 1602, a man named Cuthbert Pearson Foster, residing in the parish of St. Nicholas, Durham, was brought before the Ecclesiastical Court, charged with " playing at nine-holes upon the Sabbath day in time of divine service," and was condemned to stand once in the parish church during service, clad in a white sheet. In the following year, the four church-wardens—Rowland Swinburn, William Harp, Richard Surtees, and Cuthbert Dixon, men esteemed in Durham, and holding good positions —were found guilty and admonished for a serious breach of duty, " for not searching who was absent from the church on the Sabbath and festive days, for it is credibly reported that drinking, banqueting, and playing at cards, and other lawless games, are used in their parish in alehouses, and they never made search thereof."

Of persons in the humble ranks of life who have performed public penance in white sheets in churches, for unchastity, there are numerous entries in parish registers. For immorality, prior to marriage, man and wife were sometimes obliged to do penance. The Rev. Dr. J. Charles Cox found particulars of a case of this kind recorded in the Wooley MSS., in the British Museum, where a married couple, in the reign of James I., performed penance in Wirksworth Church.

In parish registers are records like the following, drawn from the Roxby (Lincolnshire) parish register : " Memorandum.—Michael Kirkby and Dixon, Wid. had 2 Bastard Children, one in 1725, ye other in 1727, for which they did publick pennance in our P'ish Church." " Michael Kirkby and Anne Dixon, both together did publick penance in our Parish Churche, Feb. ye 25th, 1727, for adultery."

A memorandum in the parish register of North Aston, Oxfordshire, states : " That Mr. Cooper sent in a form of penance by Mr. Wakefield, of Deddington, that Catherine King should do penance in ye parish church of North Aston, ye sixth day of March, 1740, and accordingly she did. Witness, Will Vaughan, Charles May, John Baillis, Churchwardens." We learn from the same records that another person, who had become a mother before she was made a wife, left the parish to avoid doing public penance.

Mr. John W. Walker, F.S.A., in his " History of Wakefield Cathedral," reproduces from the old churchwardens' accounts, several items bearing on this subject and amongst the number are the following :

	£	s.	d.
1679.—To Jos. Green for black bess penanc sheet...	00	05	06
1709.—Allowed the Parish Churchwardens for goeing to Leeds with ye man and woman to doe penance	0	5	0
1725.—June 13. Paid Jno. Briggs for the Lent of 3 sheets for 3 persons to do pennance ...	00	01	6
1731.—Nov. 6. Paid for the loan of two white Sheets			6
1732.—Oct. 8. Pd. for the loan of 7 sheets for penances		1	9
1735.—Nov. 1. Pd. for a sheet that —— had to do penance in		1	0
1736.—Sep. 27. Pd. for two sheets ye women did penans in...			8

		s.	d.
1736.—Oct. 10. Pd. for a sheet for Stringer to do penance in			4
1737.—June 23. Pd. for a sheet for Eliza Redhead penance			4
1750.—Dec. 26. To Priestley for a sheet & attending a woman's penance		5	0

"On February 27th, 1815," says Mr. Walker, "William Hepworth, a shoemaker, did penance in the Parish Church for defaming the character of an old woman named Elizabeth Blacketer. They both lived in Cock and Swan Yard, Westgate, and the suit was carried on by one George Robinson, an attorney, out of spite to the cobbler."

"On Sunday, August 25th, 1850, a penance was performed in the Parish Church, by sentence of the Ecclesiastical Court, on a person who had defamed the character of a lady in Wakefield. A recantation was repeated by the penitent after the Vicar, and then signed by the interested parties."

The historian of Cleveland, Mr. George Markham Tweddell, furnishes us with a copy of a document enjoining penance to be performed in 1766, by James Beadnell, of Stokesley, in the diocese of York, tailor : "The said James Beadnell shall be present in the Parish Church of Stokesley, aforesaid, upon Sunday, being the fifth, twelfth, and nineteenth day of January instant, in the time of Divine service, between the hours of ten and eleven in the forenoon of the same day, in the presence of the whole congregation then assembled, being barehead, barefoot, and barelegged, having a white sheet wrapped about him from the shoulder to the feet, and a white wand in his hand, where, immediately after the reading of the Gospel, he shall stand upon some form or seat, before the pulpit or place where the minister readeth prayers, and say after him as forthwith : ' Whereas, I, good people, forgetting my duty to Almighty God, have committed the detestable sin of adultery with Ann Andrewes, and thereby have provoked the heavy wrath of God against me to the great danger of my soul and evil example of others. I do earnestly repent, and am heartily sorry for the same, desiring Almighty God, for the merits of Jesus Christ, to forgive me both this and all other my offences, and also ever hereafter so to assist me with His Holy Spirit, that I never fall into the like offence again ; and for that end and purpose, I desire you all here present to pray for me, saying, Our Father, which art in heaven, and so forth."

Towards the close of the last century, it was the practice of women doing penance at Poulton Church, Lancashire, to pass along the aisles barefooted, clothed in a white sheet, and having in each hand a lighted candle. The last time the ceremony was performed, we are told, the cries of the poor girl melted the heart of the people, and the well-disposed raised a clamour against it, and caused the practice to be discontinued.

The Rev. Thomas Jackson, the popular Wesleyan minister, was born at Sancton, a village on the Yorkshire Wolds, in 1783. Writing of his earlier years spent in his native village, he describes two cases of public penance which he witnessed. " A farmer's son," says Mr. Jackson, " the father of an illegitimate child, came into church at the time of divine service, on the Lord's day, covered with a sheet, having a white wand in his hand ; he walked barefoot up the aisle, stood over against the desk where the prayers were read, and then repeated a confession at the dictation of the clergyman, after which he walked out of the church. The other case was that of a young woman,

' Who bore unhusbanded a mother's name.'

She also came into the church barefoot, covered
with a sheet, bearing a white wand, and went
through the same ceremony. She had one
advantage which the young man had not. Her
long hair so completely covered her face that not
a feature could be seen. In a large town, few
persons would have known who she was, but in a
small village every one is known, and no public
delinquent can escape observation, and the cen-
sure of busy tongues. These appear to have been
the last cases of the kind that occurred at
Sancton. The sin was perpetuated, but the
penalty ceased ; my father observed that the rich
offenders evaded the law, and then the authorities
could not for shame continue to inflict its penalty
upon the labouring classes."

In the month of April, 1849, penance was
performed at Ditton Church, Cambridge.

Repentance=Stool.

THE records of church-life in Scotland, in bygone times, contain many allusions to the repentance-stool. A very good specimen of this old-time relic may be seen in the Museum of the Society of Antiquaries, at Edinburgh. It is from the church of Old Greyfriars, of Edinburgh. In the same museum is a sackcloth, or gown of repentance, formerly used at the parish church of West Calder.

Persons guilty of adultery were frequently placed on the repentance-stool, and rebuked before the congregations assembled for public worship. The ordeal was a most trying one. Severe laws have been passed in Scotland to check adultery. " In the First Book of Discipline," says the Rev. Charles Rogers, LL.D., "the Reformers demanded that adulterers should be put to death. Their desire was not fully complied with, but in 1563 Parliament enacted that 'notour adulterers'—meaning those of whose illicit connection a child had been born—should be executed." Dr. Rogers and other authorities assert that the penalty was occasionally inflicted.

Paul Methven, minister at Jedburgh, in the year 1663, admitted that he had been guilty of adultery. The General Assembly conferred with the Lords of the Council respecting his conduct.

REPENTANCE-STOOL, FROM OLD GREYFRIARS, EDINBURGH.

Three years later, we are told, that he was "permitted to prostrate himself on the floor of the Assembly, and with weeping and howling to entreat for pardon." His sentence was as follows: "That in Edinburgh as the capital, in Dundee, as his native town, and in Jedburgh, the scene of his ministrations, he should stand in

sackcloth at the church door, also on the repentance-stool, and for two Sundays in each place."

A man, on his own confession, was tried for
adultery at the Presbytery of Paisley, on
November 16th, 1626, and directed "to stand and
abyde six Sabbaths barefooted and barelegged at
the kirk-door of Paisley between the second and
third bell-ringing, and thereafter to goe to the
place of public repentance during the said space
of six Sabbaths."

At Stow, in 1627, for a similar crime a man
was condemned to "sittin' eighteen dyetts" upon
the stool of repentance. Particulars of many
cases similar to the foregoing may be found in the
pages of "Social Life in Scotland," by the Rev.
Charles Rogers, in "Old Church Life in Scotland," by the Rev. Andrew Edgar, and in other
works.

Notes bearing on this subject sometimes find
their way into the newspapers, and a couple of
paragraphs from the *Liverpool Mercury* may be
quoted. On November 18th, 1876, it was stated
that "in a church in the Black Isle, Ross-shire, on
a recent Sunday, a woman who had been guilty of
transgressing the seventh commandment was
condemned to the 'cutty-stool,' and sat during

the whole service with a black shawl thrown over her head." A note in the issue for 22nd February, 1884, says that "one of the ringleaders in the Sabbatarian riots at Strome Ferry, in June last, was recently publicly rebuked and admonished on the ' cutty-stool,' in the Free Church, Lochcarron, for an offence against the moral code, which, according to Free Church discipline in the Highlands, could not be expiated in any other way."

Riding the Stang.

THE ancient custom of riding the stang still lingers in some remote parts of the country. Holding delinquents up to ridicule was a favourite mode of punishment practiced by our forefathers, and riding the stang was the means generally employed for punishing husbands who beat their wives, or allowed themselves to be henpecked, or if their conduct was deemed profligate. There are various designations for the custom. In Yorkshire, riding the stang is the name used; in Scotland the same term is applied; in the South of England skimmington-riding is the title generally employed, and on the Continent it is known by other appellations.

The mode of carrying out the ceremony is as follows: A man, having beaten his wife, the young men of the village assume the attitude of public censors, and arrangements are made for riding the stang three nights in succession. A trumpeter blows his horn loud and long as day gives way to night, and the villagers are brought together. A pole or a ladder is procured, and the most witty man in the village is placed thereon, mounted shoulder-high, and carried in great state through the streets. In one hand he has a large

RIDING THE STANG.

key or stick, and in the other a dripping-pan, and leads the music of the crowd. Men, women, and children join in the fun, and beat kettles, pans, pots, or anything else that will make a noise; tin whistles, horns, and trumpets are blown, the noise produced being better imagined than described. As soon as all is ready, a start is made, and about every fifty yards the procession stops, and the mounted man proclaims at the top of his voice a rhyme suited to the nature of the offence, somewhat as follows :

> " Ran, tan, tan ; ran, tan, tan,
>   To the sound of this pan ;
>   This is to give notice that Tom Trotter
>   Has beaten his good wo-man !
>   For what, and for why ?
>   Because she ate when she was hungry,
>   And drank when she was dry.
>   Ran, tan, ran, tan, tan ;
>   Hurrah—hurrah ! for this good wo-man !
>   He beat her, he beat her, he beat her indeed,
>   For spending a penny when she had need.
>   He beat her black, he beat her blue ;
>   When Old Nick gets him, he'll give him his due ;
>   Ran, tan, tan ; ran, tan, tan ;
>   We'll send him there in this old frying-pan ;
>   Hurrah—hurrah ! for his good wo-man ! "

Here is another version of the rhyme, jotted down in Upper Wharfedale, Yorkshire :

> " Heigh dilly, how dilly, heigh dilly dang,
>   It's naether for thy part nor my part
>   That I ride the stang ;
>   But it is for Jack Soloman—
>   His wife he does bang.
>   He bang'd her, he bang'd her,
>   He bang'd her indeed ;
>   He bang'd t' poor woman,

Though shoo stood him na need;
He naether tuke stick, staen, wire, nor stower,
But he up wi' a besom and knocked her ower.
So all ye good nahbers, who live in this row,
I pray ye tak warning for this is our law;
And all ye cross husbands
Who do your wife bang,
We'll blow for ye t' horn,
And ride for ye t' stang,
Hip, hip, hip, hurrah!"

We have an example noted at Sutton, near
Hull, in August, 1877. It was given with great
spirit by a youth, mounted after the customary
manner on a ladder, to the evident enjoyment
of a large gathering of the inhabitants, who were
enraged at the brutal treatment of a woman by
her husband:

"Here we come with a ran, dan, dang:
It's not for you, nor for me, we ride this stang;
But for ———, whose wife he did bang.
He banged her, he banged her, he banged her indeed:
He banged her, poor creature, before she stood need.
He took up neither tipstaff nor stower,
But with his fist he knocked her backwards ower;
He kicked her, he punched her, till he made her cry,
And to finish all, he gave her a black eye.
Now, all you good people that live in this row
We would have you take warning, for this is our law:
If any of you, your wives you do bang,
We're sure, we're sure, to ride you the stang."

"Last night," says the *Sunderland Daily Post*

of March 1st, 1887, "some excitement was caused in Northallerton by the celebration of the old custom of 'riding the stang,' which is to expose some one guilty of gross immoral practices, and of a breach of sacred matrimonial rights. Some hundreds of people followed the conveyance, in which two effigies were erected and exhibited through the principal streets. At intervals, a person in the conveyance shouted out in rhyme their object, and said they fully intended to make a complete celebration of the custom, which is to 'ride the stang' three nights in succession, and on the last night to burn the effigies on the green near the church."

The stang was ridden at the ancient town of Hedon, 18th, 19th, and 20th, 1889.

The house of the culprit is visited several times each night, and the proceedings kept up three nights in succession, and a circuit of the church is also made, as it is believed that those taking part in the ceremony will not be amenable to the law, if they do not omit this part of the custom. If the offence is a very serious one, the offender is burnt in effigy before his own door. In the olden days, the offender himself was often compelled to ride the stang.

Several of the old poets refer to this ancient usage. Allan Ramsay, in his poems, published in 1721, says :

> " They frae a barn a kaber raught
> And mounted wi' a bang,
> Betwisht twa's shoulders, and sat straught
> Upon't, and *rade the stang*
> *On her* that day."

Mr. Geo. Roberts, of Lyme Regis, forwarded to Sir Walter Scott some interesting notes on skimmington-riding. He wrote Sir Walter, that in the South of England : " About dusk two individuals, one armed with a skimmer and the other with a ladle, come out of some obscure street attended by a crowd, whose laughter, huzzas, etc., emulate the well-known *charivari* of the French. The two performers are sometimes in a cart, at other times on a donkey ; one personating the wife, the other the husband. They beat each other furiously with the culinary weapons above described, and, warmed by the applause and presence of so many spectators (for all turn out to see a skimmington), their dialogue attains a freedom, except using surnames, only comparable with their gestures. On arriving at the house of the parties represented in this moving drama, animation is at its height : the crowd usually stay at the spot some minutes, and then traverse the town. The performers are remunerated by the spectators : the parties who parade the streets with the performers sweep with brooms the doors of those who are likely to require a similar visitation."

Dr. King, in his "Miscellany," thus refers to the subject :

> " When the young people ride the skimmington,
> There is a general trembling in the town ;
> Not only he for whom the party rides
> Suffers, but they sweep other doors besides ;
> And by the hieroglyphic does appear
> That the good woman is the master there."

According to Douce, *skimmington* is derived from *skimming-ladle,* used in the ceremony.

In Butler's " Hudibras," considerable attention is paid to the custom. A few of the lines are as follow :

> " And now the cause of all their fear,
> By slow degrees approached so near,
> Of horns, and pans, and dogs, and boys,
> And kettle-drums whose sullen dub,
> Sounds like the hooping of a tub ;
>
> .   .   .   .   .   .
>
> And followed with a world of tall lads,
> That merry ditties troll'd and ballads.
>
> .   .   .   .   .   .

Next pans and kettles of all keys,
From trebles down to double base :

   .   .   .   .   .   .

And at fit periods the whole rout
Set up their throat with clamorous shout."

A notice of an old Welsh ceremony appeared in
the *Liverpool Mercury* on March 15th, 1887, and
it will not be without interest to reproduce it.
" That ancient Welsh custom," says the writer,
" now nearly obsolete, known as riding the ceffyl
pren—*Anglicé,* ' wooden-horse'—and intended to
operate as a wholesome warning to faithless wives
and husbands, was revived on Saturday night in
an Anglesey village some three miles from
Llangefni. The individual who had drawn upon
himself the odium of his neighbours had parted
from his wife, and was alleged to be persistent
in his attentions to another female. On Saturday night a large party surrounded the house,
and compelled him to get astride a ladder, carrying him shoulder-high through the village,
stopping at certain points to allow the woman-
kind to wreak their vengeance upon him. This
amusement was kept up for some time until the
opportune arrival of a sergeant of police from
Llangefni, who rescued the unlucky wight."

Gibbet Lore.

UNDER this heading we propose placing before the reader facts of a curious character, chiefly relating to the various modes of execution in past times. In bygone days, capital punishment formed an important feature in the everyday life, and was resorted to much more than it now is, for in those "good old times" little regard was paid for human life. People were executed for slight offences. The painful story related by Charles Dickens, in the preface to "Barnaby Rudge," is an example of many which might be mentioned. It appears that the husband of a young woman had been taken from her by the press-gang, and that she, in a time of sore distress, with a babe at her breast, was caught stealing a shilling's worth of lace from a shop in Ludgate Hill, London. The poor woman was tried, found guilty of the offence, and suffered death on the gallows. During a recent visit to the ancient burial ground of St. Mary's Church,

Bury St. Edmunds, we copied the following epitaph, which relates a painful story :

Reader,
Pause at this humble stone, it records
The fall of unguarded youth by the allurements of
vice and the treacherous snares of seduction.
SARAH LLOYD,
On the 23rd April, 1800, in the 22nd year of her age,
Suffered a just and ignominious death.
For admitting her abandoned seducer into the
dwelling-house of her mistress, on the 3rd of
October, 1799, and becoming the instrument in
his hands of the crime of robbery and
housebreaking.
These were her last words :
" May my example be a warning to thousands."

We will now deal with some of the more important modes of execution in this country.

Drowning.

Amongst the nations of antiquity, drowning was a common mode of punishment. It has only been discontinued in recent times in Europe. Four-and-a-half centuries before the birth of Christ, the Britons inflicted death by drowning in a quagmire. Women, in Anglo-Saxon times, who were found guilty of theft, were drowned. For a long period in the middle ages, the barons and others, who had the power of administering laws in their respective districts, possessed a drowning-pit and a gallows. Drowning was a punishment of King Richard of the Lion Heart, who ordained by a charter that it should be the doom of any soldier of his army who killed a fellow-crusader during the passage to the Holy Land. It was not infrequently awarded as a matter of leniency, and as a commutation of what were considered more severe forms of death. Such a case is on record for Scotland, in 1556, when a man who had been found guilty of theft and sacrilege, was ordered to be put to death by drowning, "by the Queen's special grace." The punishment in England had become obsolete by about the beginning of the seventeenth century. At Edinburgh, in 1611, a man was drowned for stealing a lamb. On the 11th May, 1685, Margaret M'Lachlan, aged sixty-three years, and Margaret Wilson, a girl of eighteen years, were drowned in the waters of Blednoch, for denying that James VII. of Scotland was entitled to rule the Church according to his pleasure. Six years prior to this, namely, on the 25th August, 1679, a woman called Janet Grant was tried for theft, in the baronial court of Sir Robert Gordon, of Gordonston, held at

Drainie, and pleaded guilty. She was sentenced to be drowned next day in the Loch of Spynie.

Bearing on this subject there is an important statement in Boys's "History of Sandwich." It is recorded that, in the year 1313, "a present-ment was made before the itinerant Justices at Canterbury that the prior of Christ Church had for nine years obstructed the high road leading from Dover Castle to Sand-wich by the sea-shore, by a water-mill, and the diversion of a stream called the Gestlyng, where felons condemned to death within the hundred should be drowned, but could not be executed that way for want of water. Further, that he raised a certain gutter four feet, and the water that passed that way to the gutter ran to the place where the convicts were drowned, and from whence their bodies were floated to the river; and that after the gutter was raised the drowned bodies could not be carried into the river by the stream, as they used to be, for want of water."

Burning to Death.

Burning to death was a frequent method of punishment in the barbarous days of many nations. In our own country, it was commonly

used by the Anglo-Saxons as the penalty of
certain crimes, and, as the ordinary punishment of
witchcraft, was maintained throughout the Middle
Ages.   Burning alive was from early times the
recognised method of uprooting heretical notions
of religious belief of every class.   The first to
suffer from this cause in England was Alban, who
died at the stake in the year A.D. 304.   Since
his day, thousands have suffered death on account
of religious belief, through religious intolerance;
but that is not a subject we intend dealing with
at the present time.   We desire to direct attention to some of the cases of the burning alive of
women for civil offences.   This practice was considered by the framers of the law as a commutation of the sentence of hanging, and a concession
made to the sin of the offenders.   Concerning
this, Sir William Blackstone writes : " For as the
decency due to the sex forbids the exposing and
publicly mangling their bodies, their sentence
(which is to the full as terrible to sensation as the
other) is, to be drawn to the gallows, and there
to be burnt alive;" and he adds : " the
humanity of the English nation has authorised,
by a tacit consent, an almost general mitigation
of such part of these judgments as savours of

torture and cruelty, a sledge or hurdle being usually allowed to such traitors as are condemned to be drawn, and there being very few instances (and those accidental and by negligence) of any persons being disemboweled or burnt till previously deprived of sensation by strangling."

We gather from the annals of King's Lynn, that in the year 1515, a woman was burnt in the market-place for the murder of her husband. Twenty years later, a Dutchman was burnt for reputed heresy. In the same town, in 1590, Margaret Read was burnt for witchcraft. Eight years later, another woman was executed for witchcraft, and in the year 1616, another woman suffered death for the same crime. In 1791, at King's Lynn, the landlady of a public-house was murdered by a man let into the house at the dead of night by a servant girl. The man was hanged for committing the crime, and the girl was burnt at the stake for assisting the murderer to enter the dwelling.

There is an account of a burning at Lincoln, in 1722. Eleanor Elsom was condemned to death for the murder of her husband, and was ordered to be burnt at the stake. She was clothed in a cloth, "made like a shift," saturated with tar, and

her limbs were also smeared with the same
inflammable substance, while a tarred bonnet had
been placed on her head.   She was brought out
of the prison barefoot, and, being put on a hurdle,
was drawn on a sledge to the place of execution
near the gallows.   Upon arrival, some time was
passed in prayer, after which the executioner
placed her on a tar barrel, a height of three feet,
against the stake.   A rope ran through a pulley
in the stake, and was placed around her neck.
she herself fixing it with her hands.   Three irons
also held her body to the stake, and the rope
being pulled tight, the tar barrel was taken aside
and the fire lighted.   The account in the "Lincoln
Date Book" states that she was probably quite
dead before the fire reached her, as the executioner pulled upon the rope several times whilst
the irons were being fixed.   The body was seen
amid the flames for nearly half-an-hour, though,
through the dryness of the wood and the
quantity of tar, the fire was exceedingly fierce.

An example where the negligence of the
executioner caused death to be unnecessarily
prolonged is the case of Catherine Hayes, who
was executed at Tyburn, November 3rd, 1726,
for the murder of her husband.   She was being

strangled in the accustomed manner, but the fire scorching the hands of the executioner, he relaxed the rope before she had become unconscious, and in spite of the efforts at once made to hasten combustion, she suffered for a considerable time the greatest agonies.

Two paragraphs, dealing with such cases, are in the *London Magazine* for July, 1735, and are as follow : " At the assizes, at Northampton, Mary Fasson was condemned to be burnt for poisoning her husband, and Elizabeth Wilson to be hanged for picking a farmer's pocket of thirty shillings."

" Among the persons capitally convicted at the assizes, at Chelmsford, are Herbert Hayns, one of Gregory's gang, who is to be hung in chains, and a woman for poisoning her husband is to be burnt."

In the next number of the same magazine, the first-mentioned criminal is again spoken of : " Mrs. Fasson was burnt at Northampton for poisoning her husband. Her behaviour in prison was with the utmost signs of contrition. She would not, to satisfy people's curiosity, be unveiled to anyone. She confessed the justice of her sentence, and died with great composure of mind." And also : " Margaret Onion was burnt at a stake at Chelmsford, for poisoning her husband. She was a poor, ignorant creature, and confessed the fact."

In the "New Suffolk Garland," there are some particulars of another case of burning for husband murder (styled petty treason). In April, 1763, Margaret Beddington, and a farm servant, named Richard Ringe, her paramour, had murdered John Beddingfield, of Sternfield. The latter criminal was the actual murderer, the wife being considered an accomplice. He was condemned to be hanged and she burnt, at the same time and place, and her sentence was that she should " be taken from hence to the place from whence you came, and thence to the place of execution, on Saturday next, where you are to be burnt until you be dead; and the Lord have mercy on your soul." Accordingly, on the day appointed, she was taken to Rushmere Heath, near Ipswich, and there strangled and burnt.

Coining was, until a late period, an offence which met with capital punishment. In Harrison's *Derby and Nottingham Journal, or Midland Advertiser*, for September 23rd, 1779, is an account of two persons who were, several days previously, tried and convicted for high treason, the indictment being for coining shillings in Cold Bath Field, and for coining shillings in Nag's Head Yard, Bishopgate Street. The culprit in the latter case was a man named John Fields, and in the former a woman named Isabella Condon. They were sentenced to be drawn on a hurdle to the place of execution, where the man was hanged, and the woman burnt.

In the pages of the *Quarterly Review* are particulars of burning alive for coining offences. It appears that a girl of little more than fourteen years of age had, at her master's command, concealed a number of whitewashed counters behind her stays, for which she was found guilty of treason, and sentenced to be executed by the barbarous method we have described. Her master was already hanged, and the fagots but awaiting the application of the match to blaze in fury around her when Lord Weymouth, who happened to be passing that way, humanely interfered. As the *Review* says : " mere accident saved the nation from this crime and this national disgrace." But such things awakened little public attention in that day, though the case above mentioned was discussed in Parliament, and, among others, by Sir William Meredith. The last execution in front of Newgate, by burning, was about 1786, when a woman was hanged on a low gibbet ; and, when life was extinct, fagots were piled around and over her, and fire was put to the pyre, and the body was burnt to ashes. The latest instance on record is that of a woman named Christian Murphy, *alias* Bowman, who was burnt on March 18th, 1789, for coining. The barbarous laws which permitted such repugnant exhibitions were repealed by the 30th George III., cap. 48, which provided that, after the 5th of June, 1790, women were to suffer hanging, as in the case of men.

Boiling to Death.

Boiling to death was a legal punishment in the olden time, though instances of its exercise were not so frequent in the annals of crime as some of the other modes of execution. In the year 1531, when Henry VIII. was King, an Act was passed for boiling poisoners to death. The Act details the case of one Richard Roose, or Coke, a cook in the diocese of the Bishop of Rochester, who had, by putting poison in the food of several persons, occasioned the death of two, and the serious illness of others. He was found guilty of treason, and sentenced to be boiled to death without benefit of clergy; that is, that no abatement of sentence was to be made on account of his ecclesiastical connection, nor to be allowed any indemnity such as was commonly the privilege of clerical offenders. He was brought to punishment at Smithfield, on the 15th of April, 1532; and the Act ordained that all manner of poisoners should meet with the same doom henceforth. A maid-servant, in 1531, was boiled to death in the market-place of King's Lynn, for the crime of poisoning her mistress. Margaret Davy, a maid-servant, for poisoning persons with whom she had lived, perished at Smithfield on March 28th, 1542. The Act was repealed in the year 1547.

The punishment had been common both in England and on the Continent before its precise enforcement by Henry's Act. It has frequent mention as a punishment for coining. The "Chronicle of the Grey Friars of London" (published by the Camden Society) has an account of a case at Smithfield, in which a man was fastened to a chain and let down into the boiling water several times until he was dead.

Beheading.

Beheading, as a mode of punishment, has an early origin. Amongst the Romans it was regarded as a most honourable death. It is asserted that it was introduced into England from Normandy by William the Conqueror, and intended for putting to death of criminals belonging to the higher grades of mankind. The first person to suffer beheading was Waltheof, Earl of Huntingdon, Northampton, and Northumberland, in 1076. Since that year, some of the leading members of the English nobility have perished at the block. An early victim of the axe was William Wallace, of illustrious memory, who was beheaded on a scaffold at the Elms, at Smithfield, in 1305. But at this later period, beheading by sword or axe had become the established mode of punishment for theft. Murder, it may be remarked, was punished by outlawry, but theft of goods and cattle by death ; while in the Isle of Man the stealing of a beast was only considered trespass, but the stealing of a fowl was death. The duration of decapitation as an English punishment in ordinary use may be considered to have been from about the middle, probably, of the twelfth century to the middle and end of the fourteenth century. The long list of beheaded includes several queens and noble ladies, famous for grace, wit, and beauty, and ends with Lord Lovat, who was

AXE, BLOCK, AND EXECUTIONER'S MASK AT THE TOWER OF LONDON.

beheaded on the 9th April, 1747, for espousing the Pretender's cause.

Hanging, Drawing, and Quartering.

Hanging, drawing, and quartering, with their attendant horrors, have been termed "godly butchery," on account of the divine authority which was adduced to support their continuance.

Lord Coke finds in the Bible a countenance for each of the horrid details of the punishment. We see that the texts supposed to bear upon the subject are raked from all parts of the Scriptures with great ingenuity, but with, in our modern eyes, not much of either humanity or probability of there being anything more than a forced reference. The sentence on traitors was pronounced as follows : " That the traitor is to be taken from the prison and laid upon a sledge or hurdle [in earlier days he was to be dragged along the surface of the ground, tied to the tail of a horse], and drawn to the gallows or place of execution, and then hanged by the neck until he be half dead, and then cut down ; and his entrails to be cut out of his body and burnt by the executioner; then his head is to be cut off, his body to be divided into quarters, and afterwards his head and quarters to be set up in some open places directed." The headsman, or hangsman commonly, sliced open the chest and cut thence the heart, plucking it forth and holding it up to the populace, saying, " Behold the heart of a traitor." The members were disposed on the gates of the cities, and in London on London Bridge, or upon Westminster Hall.

It is stated that this kind of punishment was first inflicted in the year 1241, on William Marise, pirate, and the son of a nobleman. On the 1st May, 1820, the Cato Street Conspirators were beheaded after death by hanging.

We must not omit to state that the great agitator against the continuance of the barbarities of hanging, drawing, and quartering was Sir Samuel Romilly, who, in the reign of George III. (for so late did this disgrace to England continue), brought upon himself the odium of the law officers of the Crown, who declared he was "breaking down the bulwarks of the constitution." By his earnest exertions, however, the punishment was carried out in a manner much more amenable to the dictates of mercy and humanity.

Pressing to Death.

One of the most barbarous and cruel of the punishments of our English statutes was that distinguished by the name of *Peine forte et dure*, or pressing to death with every aggravation of torture. It was adopted as a manner of punishment suitable to cases where the accused refused to plead, and was commuted in the year 1406, from the older method of merely starving the prisoner to death. At that time the alteration was considered to be decidedly according to the dictates of humanity and mercy, as the sooner relieving the accused from his sufferings. Such was the small value set upon human life in those dark days of British justice. The manner in which this exceedingly great torture was inflicted was as follows : " That the prisoner shall be remanded to the place from whence he came, and put in some low, dark room, and there laid on his back, without any manner of covering except a cloth round his middle ; and that as many weights shall be laid upon him as he can bear, *and more;* and that he shall have no more sustenance but of the worst bread and water, and that he shall not eat the same day on which he drinks, nor drink the same day on which he eats ; and he shall so continue till he die." At a later period, the form of sentence was altered to the following : " That the prisoner shall be remanded to the place from whence he came, and put in some low, dark room, that he shall lie without any litter or anything under him, and that one arm shall be drawn to one quarter of the room with a cord, and the other to another, and that his feet shall be used in the same manner, and that as many weights shall be laid on him as he can bear, and more. That he shall have three morsels of barley bread a day, and that he shall have the water next the prison, so that it be not current, and that he shall not eat," etc. The object of this protracted punishment was to allow the victim, at almost every stage of the torture, to plead, and thus allow the law to take its ordinary course. The object of the persons who have refused to plead is, that any person who dies under the *Peine forte et dure* can transmit his estates to his children, or will them as he desires; whereas, if he were found guilty, they would be forfeited to the Crown. In connection with this, it may be mentioned that when the practice of pressing to death had become nearly extinct, prisoners who declined to plead were tortured in order to compel them to do so, by twisting and screwing their thumbs with whipcord. In 1721, a woman named Mary Andrews was subjected to this punishment. After bearing with fortitude the first three whipcords, which broke from the violence of the twisting, she submitted to plead at the fourth. Baron Carter, at the Cambridge Assizes, in 1741, ordered a prisoner, who refused to plead, to have his thumbs twisted with cords, and when that was without avail, inflicted the higher penalty of pressing. Baron Thompson, about the same time, at the Sussex Assizes, treated a prisoner in a precisely similar manner. In 1721 also, a like method was pursued with Nathaniel Hawes, a prisoner who refused to plead; when the cord proved inefficacious, a weight of 250 pounds was laid upon him, after which he decided to plead. In the same year also, which seems prolific of cases of this character, there are particulars of an instance to be found in the *Nottingham Mercury* of January 19th, 1721. They are included in the London news, and are as follow : " Yesterday the sessions began at the Old Bailey, where several persons were brought to the bar for the highway, etc. Among them were the highway-men lately taken at Westminster, two of whom, namely, Thomas Green, *alias* Phillips, and Thomas Spigot, refusing to plead, the court proceeded to pass the following sentence upon them : 'that the prisoner shall be,' etc. [the usual form, as given above]. The former, on sight of the terrible machine, desired to be carried back to the sessions house, where he pleaded not guilty. But the other, who behaved

himself very insolently to the ordinary who was
ordered to attend him, seemingly resolved to
undergo the torture. Accordingly, when they
brought cords, as usual, to tie him, he broke
them three several times like a twine-thread, and
told them if they brought cables he would serve
them after the same manner. But, however,
they found means to tie him to the ground,
having his limbs extended; but, after enduring
the punishment for an hour, and having three or
four hundredweight put on him, he at last submitted to plead, and was carried back, when he
pleaded not guilty." The Rev. Mr. Willette,
with the ordinary of the prison, in 1776,
published the "Annals of Newgate," and from
these we learn further particulars of the torture
of the highwayman, Spigot. "The chaplain
found him lying in the vault upon the bare
ground, with 350 pounds weight upon his breast,
and then prayed with him, and at several times
asked him why he should hazard his soul by such
obstinate kind of self-murder. But all the
answer that he made was, 'Pray for me; pray for
me.' He sometimes lay silent under the pressure
as if insensible to the pain, and then again would
fetch his breath very quick and short. Several

times he complained that they had laid a cruel weight upon his face, though it was covered with nothing but a thin cloth, which was afterwards removed and laid more light and hollow; yet he still complained of the prodigious weight upon his face, which might be caused by the blood being forced up thither and pressing the veins so violently as if the force had been externally on his face. When he had remained for half-an-hour under this load, and fifty pounds weight more laid on, being in all four hundred, he told those who attended him he would plead. The weights were at once taken off, the cords cut asunder; he was raised up by two men, some brandy put into his mouth to revive him, and he was carried to take his trial." The practice of *Peine forte et dure* gave the name of "Press-yard" to a part of Newgate, and the terrible machine above referred to was probably in the form of rack. We require to go further back to find instances of fatal termination to the punishment. Such a case occurred in 1676. One Major Strangeways and his sister held in joint possession a farm, but the lady, becoming intimate with a lawyer named Fussell, to whom the Major took a strong dislike, he threatened that if she married the lawyer he would, in his office or elsewhere, be the death of him. Surely, Fussell was one day found shot dead in his London apartments, and suspicion at once fell upon the soldier, and he was arrested. At first he was willing to be subjected to the ordeal of touch, but when placed upon trial, resolved not to allow any chance of his being found guilty, and so refused to plead, in order that his estates might go to whom he willed. Glynn was the Lord Chief Justice on this occasion, and in passing the usual sentence for *Peine forte et dure*, used instead of the word "weights," as above, the words "as much iron and stone as he can bear," doubtless to suit the prison convenience, and make the sentence perfectly legal. He was to have three morsels of barley bread every alternate day, and three draughts of "the water in the next channel to the prison door, but of no spring or fountain water," the sentence concluding, "and this shall be his punishment till he die." This was probably on the Saturday, for on the Monday morning following, it is stated, the condemned was draped in white garments, and also wore a mourning cloak, as though in mourning for his own forthcoming death. It is curious to notice that his friends were present at his death, which was much modified from the lengthy process that his sentence conveys, as to be in fact an execution, in which these same friends assisted. They stood "at the corner of the press," and when he gave them to understand that he was ready, they forthwith proceeded to pile stone and iron upon him. The amount of weight was insufficient to kill him, for although he gasped, "Lord Jesus, receive my soul," he still continued alive until his friends, to hasten his departure, stood **upon** the weights, a course which in about ten minutes placed him beyond the reach of the human barbarity which imposed upon friendship so horrible a task.

In 1827, an Act was passed which directs the court to enter a plea of "not guilty," when a prisoner refuses to plead.

Hanging.

The usual mode of inflicting death upon criminals in Anglo-Saxon times was by hanging. In our chapter on "Whipping," we have directed attention to the cruelty of Anglo-Saxon ladies in flogging their servants and children, which is a marked contrast to the laws of the land, more

especially those relating to capital punishment.
The laws, as a rule, were mild, and contrary in
spirit to capital punishment. We draw from the
laws of Ethelred as follows : " And the ordinance
of our lord, and of his witan (parliament), is that
Christian men for all too little be condemned to
death ; but in general, let mild punishment be
decreed for the people's
need ; and let not for a little
God's own handiwork and
His own purchase be des-
troyed, which He dearly
bought." Canute, in his
laws, repealed the foregoing
injunction. We give a re-
presentation of an Anglo-
Saxon gallows *(gala)*, taken
from the illuminations to
Alfric's version of Genesis.

ANGLO-SAXON GALLOWS.

In course of time, the
gallows were very largely employed, and, in
the Middle Ages, were familiar sights in the
country. " Every town, every abbey, and almost
every large manorial lord," says Thomas Wright,
" had the right of hanging, and a gallows or
tree, with a man hanging upon it, was so fre-

quent an object in the country, that it seems to have been considered as almost a natural object of a landscape, and it is thus introduced, by no means uncommonly, in mediæval manuscripts." In the reign of Henry VI., which extended over thirty-eight years, it is stated that 72,000 criminals were executed.

In the curious ordinances which were observed in the reign of Henry VI., for the conduct of the Court of Admiralty of the Humber, are enumerated the various offences of a maritime connection, and their punishment. In view of the character of the court, the punishment was generally to be inflicted at low watermark, so as to be within the proper jurisdiction of the Admiralty, the chief officer of which, the Admiral of the Humber, being, from the year 1451, the Mayor of Hull. The court being met, and consisting of "masters, merchants, and mariners, with all others that do enjoy the King's stream with hook, net, or any engine," were addressed as follows : " You masters of the quest, if you, or any of you, discover or disclose anything of the King's secret counsel, or of the counsel of your fellows (for the present you are admitted to be the King's Counsellors), you are to be, and shall be, had down to the low water-mark, where must be made three times, O Yes! for the King, and then and there this punishment, by the law prescribed, shall be executed upon them ; that is, their hands and feet bound, their throats cut, their tongues pulled out, and their bodies thrown into the sea."

The ordinances which they were bound to observe, include the following : "You shall inquire, whether any man in port or creek, have stolen any ropes, nets, cords, etc., amounting to the value of ninepence ; if he have, he must be hanged for the said crimes, at low water-mark." "If any person has removed the anchor of any ship, without licence of the master or mariners, or both, or if anyone cuts the cable of a ship at anchor, or removes or cuts away a buoy ; for any of the said offences, he shall be hanged at low water-mark." "All breakers open of chests, or pickers of locks, coffers, or chests, etc., on shipboard, if under the value of one and twenty pence, they shall suffer forty days' imprisonment ; but, if above, they must be hanged as aforesaid." "If any loderman takes upon himself the rule of any ship, and she perishes through his carelessness and negligence, if he comes to land alive with two of his company, they two may chop off his head without any further suit with the King or his Admiralty." The sailor element of the population of the olden days was undeniably rude and refractory, the above rules showing that the authorities needed stern and swift measures to repress evildoers of that class.

The royal burgh of Wigtown had, in early days, a public executioner of its own, a privilege which was permitted it upon somewhat peculiar conditions, if the traditional accounts are to be credited. The law was that this functionary was himself to be a criminal under sentence of death, but whose doom was to be deferred until the advance of age prevented a continuance of his usefulness, and then he was to be hanged forthwith. If, it was said, the town permitted the executioner to die by the ordinary decay of nature, and not by the process of the cord, it would lose for ever the distinguished honour of possessing a public hangman. The story of the last official who held the tenure of his life upon the curious condition of his being able to efficiently despatch his fellows is sufficiently interesting. He was taken ill, and it was seriously contemplated to make sure of having a public hangman in the future by seizing the sick man and hanging him. His friends, hearing of this intention, propped the dying Ketch up in bed, and he, being by trade a shoemaker, the tools and materials of his trade were placed before him. He made a pretence of plying his avocation, and the townsmen, thinking his lease of life was in no danger of a natural termination, allowed him to lie in peace. He then speedily passed away quietly in his bed, and the outwitted burghers found themselves without a hangman, and without hope of a successor. This is how Wigtown, made a royal borough in 1341, lost its hangman. We glean the particulars of this strange story from one of Mr. Gordon Fraser's informing and entertaining historical books. He tells a good anecdote of Patrick Clanachan, executed for horse-stealing in 1709. This man was the last person hanged at Wigtown, and we are told that " the doom pronounced was 'that he be taken on the 31st August, between the hours of 12 and 2 in the afternoon, to the gyppet at Wigtown, and there to hang till he was dead.' Clanachan was carried from the prison to the gallows on a hurdle, and, as the people were hurrying on past him to see the execution, he

is said to have remarked : ' Tak' yer time, boys ;
there'll be no fun till I gang.' " A similar
story is told respecting a criminal in London.

At Wicklow, in the year 1738, a man named
George Manley was hanged for murder, and just
before his execution he delivered an address to
the crowd, as follows : " My friends, you
assemble to see—what ? A man leap into
the abyss of death ! Look, and you will
see me go with as much courage as Curtius,
when he leapt into the gulf to save his country
from destruction. What will you see of
me ? You say that no man, without virtue can
be courageous ! You see what I am—I'm a
little fellow. What is the difference between
running into a poor man's debt, and by the power
of gold, or any other privilege, prevent him from
obtaining his right, and clapping a pistol to a
man's breast, and taking from him his purse ?
Yet the one shall thereby obtain a coach, and
honours, and titles; the other, what ?—a cart and
a rope. Don't imagine from all this that I am
hardened. I acknowledge the just judgment of
God has overtaken me. My Redeemer knows
that murder was far from my heart, and what I
did was through rage and passion, being provoked

by the deceased. Take warning, my comrades;
think what would I now give that I had lived
another life. Courageous? You'll say I've
killed a man. Marlborough killed his thousands,
and Alexander his millions. Marlborough and
Alexander, and many others, who have done the
like, are famous in history for great men. Aye
—that's the case—one solitary man. I'm a little
murderer, and must be hanged. Marlborough and
Alexander plundered countries; they were great
men. I ran in debt with the ale-wife. I must
be hanged. How many men were lost in Italy,
and upon the Rhine, during the last war for
settling a king in Poland. Both sides could not
be in the right! They are great men; but I
killed a solitary man."

The following curious incident is recorded in
the *Derby Mercury* of April 6th, 1738 : " Here-
ford, March 25.—This day Will Summers
and Tipping were executed here for housebreaking. At the tree, the hangman was intoxi-
cated with liquor, and supposing that there were
three for execution, was going to put one of the
ropes round the parson's neck as he stood in the
cart, and was with much difficulty prevented by
the gaoler from so doing."

Hanging persons was almost a daily occurrence in the earlier years of the present century, for forging notes, passing forged notes, and other crimes which we now almost regard with indifference. George Cruikshank claimed with the aid of his artistic skill to have been the means of putting an end to hanging for minor offences. Cruikshank, in a letter to his friend, Mr. Whitaker, furnishes full details bearing on the subject. "About the year 1817 or 1818," wrote Cruikshank, "there were one-pound Bank of England notes in circulation, and unfortunately there were forged one-pound bank notes in circulation also; and the punishment for passing these forged notes was in some cases transportation for life, and in others DEATH.

"At that time, I resided in Dorset Street, Salisbury Square, Fleet Street, and had occasion to go early one morning to a house near the Bank of England ; and in returning home between eight or nine o'clock, down Ludgate Hill, and seeing a number of persons looking up the Old Bailey, I looked that way myself, and saw several human beings hanging on the gibbet, opposite Newgate prison, and, to my horror, two of them were women ; and upon enquiring what the women had been hung for, was informed that it was for passing forged one-pound notes. The fact that a poor woman could be put to death for such a minor offence had a great effect upon me, and I at once determined, if possible, to put a stop to this shocking destruction of life for merely obtaining a few shillings by fraud; and well knowing the habits of the low class of society in London, I felt quite sure that in very many cases the rascals who had forged the notes induced these poor ignorant women to go into the gin-shops to 'get something to drink,' and thus *pass* the notes, and hand them the change.

" My residence was a short distance from Ludgate Hill (Dorset Street); and after witnessing the tragic scene, I went home, and in ten minutes designed and made a sketch of this *'Bank-note not to be imitated.'* About half-an-hour after this was done, William Hone came into my room, and saw the sketch lying on my table; he was much struck with it, and said, ' What are you going to do with this, George ? '

" ' To publish it,' I replied. Then he said. 'Will you let me have it ?' To his request I consented, made an etching of it, and it was published. Mr. Hone then resided on Ludgate

Hill, not many yards from the spot where I had seen the people hanging on the gibbet; and when it appeared in his shop windows, it caused a great sensation, and the people gathered round his house in such numbers that the Lord Mayor had to send the City police (of that day) to disperse the CROWD. The Bank directors held a meeting immediately upon the subject, and AFTER THAT they issued *no more* one-pound notes, and so there was *no more hanging for passing* FORGED *one-pound notes;* not only that, but ultimately no hanging even for forgery. AFTER THIS Sir Robert Peel got a Bill passed in Parliament for the ' Resumption of cash payments.' AFTER THIS he revised the Penal Code, and AFTER THAT *there was not any more hanging or punishment of* DEATH *for minor offences.* " We are enabled, by the courtesy of Mr. Walter Hamilton, the author of a favourably-known life of Cruikshank, to give as a frontispiece to this volume a picture of the " Bank-note not to be imitated." In concluding his letter to Mr. Whitaker, Cruikshank said : " I consider it the most important design and etching that I ever made in my life ; for it has saved the life of thousands of my fellow-creatures ; and for having been able to do this

Christian act, I am indeed most sincerely thankful."

It will not be without historical interest to state that the last execution for attempted murder was Martin Doyle, hanged at Chester, August 27th, 1861. By the Criminal Law Consolidation Acts, passed 1861, death was confined to treason and wilful murder. The Act was passed before Doyle was put on trial, but (unfortunately for him) did not take effect until November 1st, 1861. Michael Barrett, author of the Fenian explosion at Clerkenwell, hanged at Newgate, May 26th, 1868, was the last person publicly executed in England. Thomas Wells (murderer of Mr. Walsh, station-master at Dover), hanged at Maidstone, August 13th, 1868, was the first person to be executed within a prison.

Hanging in Chains.

Gibbeting, or hanging in chains the bodies of executed criminals, near the site where their crimes were committed, was a common practice, which has come down to recent times. Blackstone, in his "Commentaries," published in 1769, has a note bearing on this subject. "In atrocious cases " [of murder], writes Blackstone, " it was frequently usual for the court to direct the murderer, after execution, to be hung upon a gibbet where the act was committed : but this was no part of the legal judgment ; and the like is still sometimes practiced in the case of notorious thieves. This, being quite contrary to the express command of the Mosaical law, seems to have been borrowed from the civil law ; which, besides the terror of the example, gives also another reason for this practice, namely, that it is a comfortable sight to the relations and friends of the deceased."

It is not an uncommon circumstance for persons to assert that, in bygone times, criminals were hanged alive in chains. It is a disputed question in the history of England. It will be observed, from the preceding quotation from the works of Blackstone, that a criminal was suspended in chains after execution. Holinshed, who died about the year 1580, in his famous " Chronicle of England," a work which supplied Shakespeare with materials for historical dramas, states : " In wilful murder done upon pretended (premeditated) malice, or in anie notable robbery, the criminal is either hanged alive in chains near the place where the act was committed, or else, upon compassion taken, first strangled with a rope, and so continueth till his bones came to nothing. Where wilful manslaughter is perpetrated, besides hanging, the offender hath his right hand commonly stricken off."

We glean an important item from " England's Mourning Garment," written by Henry Chettle, a poet and dramatist, born about the year 1540, and died in 1604. He lived in the days of Queen Elizabeth. " But for herselfe," wrote Chettle, "she was alwayes so inclined to equitie that if she left justice in any part, it was in shewing pittie; as in one generall punishment of murder it appeared: where-as before time there was extraordinary tortore, as hanging wilfull murderers alive in chains; she having compassion like a true Shepheardesse of their soules, though they were of her erring and utterly infected flock, said their death satisfied for death ; and life for life was all that could be demanded ; and affirming more, that much torture distracted a dying man."

Almost every district in England has its strange story of a man hanging alive in chains. Mr. H. T. Wake committed to writing, in 1860, at Wetherell, the following : " John Whitfield, a notorious highwayman, was gibbetted alive on

Barrock, a hill a few miles from Wetherell, near Carlisle, about the year 1777. He lived at Coathill, and was the terror to all that part of the country, so that many would not venture out after nightfall, especially along the road by Barrock. It appears that he shot a horseman in the open day, who was travelling to Armathwaite. As soon as the shot was fired, the horse galloped off, and, although the man was mortally wounded, he had sufficient strength to keep his seat till he had got nearly home, when he fell and died soon after from exhaustion. A boy who concealed himself near the place where Whitfield was shot was the means of bringing this unmerciful wretch to be identified ; a button off his coat being part of the evidence adduced It is said that he hung for several days, till his cries were heartrending, and a mail-coachman, who was passing that way, put him out of his misery by shooting him.

Terror and indignation were felt by the inhabitants of the quiet Midland town of Derby on Christmas day, in the year 1775, as the news spread through the place that, on the previous evening, an old lady had been murdered and her house plundered.

An Irishman named Matthew Cocklain disappeared from the town, and he was suspected of committing the foul deed. He was traced to his native country, arrested, and brought back to Derby. At the following March Assizes, he was tried, found guilty of committing the crime, sentenced to be hanged, and afterwards gibbeted. His body was for some time suspended in the summer sun and winter cold, an object of fright to the people in the neighbourhood.

Christmas eve had come round once more, and at a tavern, near the gibbet, a few friends were enjoying a pipe and glass around the cheerful burning yule-log, when the conversation turned to the murderer, and a wager was made that a certain member of the company dare not venture near the grim gibbet at that late hour of the night. The man agreed to go, and take with him a basin of broth and offer it to Matthew Cocklain. He proceeded without delay, carrying on his shoulder a ladder and in his hand a bowl of hot broth. On arriving at the foot of the gibbet he mounted the ladder, and put to Cocklain's mouth the basin, saying, " Sup, Matthew," but, to his great astonishment, a hollow voice replied, " It's hot." He was taken by surprise ; but, equal to the occasion, and at once said, " Blow it, blow it," subsequently throwing the liquid into the face of the suspended body.

He returned to the cosy room of the hostelry to receive the bet he had won. His mate, who had been hid behind the gibbet-post, and had tried to frighten him with his sepulchral speech, admitted that the winner was a man of nerve, and richly entitled to the wager.

In the pages of *The Antiquary* for November, 1890, are some notes on " Hanging in Chains." " It was usual," says the Rev. J. Charles Cox, " to saturate the body with tar before it was in chains, in order that it might last the longer. This was done with the bodies of three highwaymen about the middle of last century, gibbeted on the top of the Chevin, near Belper, in Derbyshire. They had robbed the North Coach when it was changing horses at the inn at Hazelwood, just below the summit of the Chevin. After the bodies had been hanging there a few weeks, one of the friends of the criminals set fire, at night time, to the big gibbet that bore all three. The father of our aged informant, and two or three others of the cottagers near by, seeing a glare of light, went up the hill, and there they saw the sickening spectacle of the three bodies blazing away in the darkness. So thoroughly did the tar aid this cremation, that the next morning only the links of the iron chain remained on the site of the gibbet."

At the Derby March Assizes, 1815, a young man, named Anthony Lingard, was tried and convicted for murder-ing Hannah Oliver, a widow who kept the turnpike-gate at Ward-low Miers, in the parish of Tideswell. In the columns of the *Derby Mercury* is a full ac-count of the trial of Lingard. "Before the judge left the town," says the report, "he directed that the body of Lingard should be

LINGARD'S GIBBET-CAP.

hung in chains in the most convenient place near the spot where the murder was committed, instead of being dissected and anatomized."

A paragraph in Rhodes' "Peak Scenery," first published in 1818, is worth reproducing. "As

we passed along the road to Tideswell," writes
Rhodes, "the villages of Wardlow and Litton lay
on our left. . . . . Here, at a little distance
on the left of the road, we observed a man
suspended on a gibbet, which was but newly
erected." The vanity of the absurd idea of our
forefathers, in thinking that a repulsive object
of this kind would act as a deterrent of crime,
was strikingly shown in the case of this Wardlow
gibbet. It is related of Hannah Pecking, of
Litton, who was hung on March 22nd, 1819, at
the early age of sixteen, for poisoning Jane Grant,
a young woman of the same village, that she
"gave the poison in a sweet cake to her
companion as they were going to fetch some
cattle out of a field near to which stood the
gibbet-post of Anthony Lingard."

Dr. J. Charles Cox, in his "Three Centuries
of Derbyshire Annals," has some important notes
bearing on Lingard's case. He states that:
"The treasurer's accounts for Derbyshire, for
1815-16, show that the gibbeting involved a
serious inroad on the county finances. The
expenses for apprehending Anthony Lingard
amounted to £31 5s. 5d.; but the expenses
incurred in gibbeting reached a total of

£85 4s. 1d., and this, in addition to ten guineas charged by the gaoler for conveying the body from Derby to Wardlow."

The gibbet was taken down on April 10th, 1826, by the order of the Magistrates, and the remains of Lingard buried on the spot. Mr. Alfred Burton favours us with a drawing of Lingard's gibbet-cap, which is now in the museum at Belle Vue, Manchester.

On the 16th April, 1889, Mr. Charles Madeley read a paper before the Warrington Literary and Philosophical Society, under the title of " Some Obsolete Modes of Punishment." His compilation includes much curious information collected from many sources, states that the last person gibbeted in the neighbourhood of Warrington was a man named Edward Miles, who murdered the postboy who was carrying the Liverpool mail-bag to Manchester, on September 15th, 1791. Miles was hanged for the crime, and afterwards his body was suspended in chains near the scene of the murder. The gibbet-irons are now in the Warrington Museum.

In the *Daily Graphic* of July 19th, 1890, is a small sketch of the irons kept in the Rye Town Hall, in which a man named John Breeds was gibbeted in 1742, for the murder of Allen Grebbell, the Mayor of Rye, in mistake for another man, with whom he had a dispute about some property.

Lincolnshire history supplies some curious details respecting the gibbeting of a man named Tom Otter, in the year 1806. We are told that he was " compelled by the old poor regulations to wed a girl he had injured. He lured her into a secluded spot the day after their marriage, and deliberately murdered her. According to the prevalent custom, Tom Otter's corpse was hung in chains. The day selected for that purpose inaugurated a week of merrymaking of the most unseemly character. Booths were pitched near the gibbet, and great numbers of people came from a distance to see the wretch suspended. It is reported that some years later, when the jaw bones had become sufficiently bare to leave a cavity between them, a bird built its nest in this unique situation. The discovery of nine young ones therein gave rise to the following triplet, still quoted in the neighbourhood :

> ' There were nine tongues within one head,
> The tenth went out to seek some bread,
> To feed the living in the dead.' "

The gibbet was standing until the year 1850, when it was blown down.

The last man gibbeted in this country was George Cook, a bookbinder, at Leicester. He was executed for the murder of a commercial traveller, from London. Cook's body was suspended on a gibbet thirty-three feet high, on Saturday, August 11th, 1832, in Saffron Lane, Aylestone, near Leicester. The body was soon taken down, and buried on the spot where the gibbet stood, by order of the Secretary of State, to put a stop to the disturbances caused by the crowds of people visiting the place on a Sunday.

The old custom of hanging the bodies of criminals in chains was abolished on July 25th, 1834, and thus ends a strange chapter in the history of Old England.

The Halifax Gibbet.

The mention of the Halifax gibbet suggests a popular Yorkshire saying, namely: "From Hell, Hull and Halifax, good Lord, deliver us." Fuller says the foregoing is part of the "Beggars' and Vagrants' Litany," and goes on to state: "Of these three frightful things unto them, it is to be feared that they least fear the first, conceiting it

the farthest from them. Hull is terrible to them
as a town of good government, where beggars
meet with punitive charity; and, it is to be feared,
are oftener corrected than amended. Halifax is
formidable for the law thereof, whereby thieves,
taken in the very act of stealing cloth, are
instantly beheaded with an engine, without any
further legal proceedings. Doubtless, the coinci-
dence of the initial letters of these three words
helped much the setting on foot of the proverb."
The Halifax gibbet law has been traced back to
a remote period. It has been suggested that it
was imported into the country by some of the
Norman barons. Holinshed's " Chronicle " (edition published in 1587) contains an interesting
note bearing on this subject. " There is, and has
been, of ancient time," says Holinshed, " a law,
or rather custom, at Halifax, that whosoever
doth commit any felony, and is taken with the
same, or confess the fact upon examination, if it
be valued by four constables to amount to the
sum of thirteenpence-halfpenny, he is forthwith
beheaded upon one of the next market-days
(which fall usually upon the Tuesdays, Thursdays,
and Saturdays), or else upon the same day that
he is convicted, if market be holden. The engine

wherewith the execution is done is a square
block of wood, of the length of four feet and a
half, which doth ride up and down in a slot, rabet,
or regall, between two pieces of timber that are
framed and set up right, of five yards in height.
In the nether end of a sliding block is an axe,
keyed or fastened with an iron into the wood,
which, being drawn up to the top of the frame,
is there fastened by a wooden pin (with a notch
made in the same, after the manner of a Samson's
post), unto the middest of which pin also there is
a long rope fastened, that cometh down among
the people ; so that when the offender hath made
his confession, and hath laid his neck over the
nethermost block, every man there present doth
either take hold of the rope (or putteth forth his
arm so near to the same as he can get, in token
that he is willing to see justice executed), and
pulling out the pin in this manner, the head-
block wherein the axe is fastened doth fall down
with such a violence, that if the neck of the
transgressor were so big as that of a bull, it
should be cut in sunder at a stroke, and roll from
the body by an huge distance. If it be so that
the offender be apprehended for an ox, sheep,
kine, horse, or any such cattle, the self beast or

HALIFAX GIBBET.

other of its kind shall have the end of the rope tied somewhere unto them, so that they being driven, do draw out the pin whereby the offender is executed."

In the picture which we give, which is a reproduction of an old illustration, it will be observed that a horse is drawing the rope to loosen the pin, and allow the axe to fall and cut off the head of the victim. The doomed man had doubtless stolen the horse. Near the gibbet are assembled the jurymen, and the parish priest is engaged in prayer.

Before a felon was condemned to suffer, the proof of certain facts appear to have been essentially necessary. In the first place, he was to be taken in the liberty of the forest of Hardwick, and if he escaped out of it, even after condemnation, he could not be brought back to be executed ; but if he ever returned into the liberty again, and was taken, he was sure to suffer. It is recorded that a man named Lacy escaped, and resided seven years out of the forest, but returning, was beheaded on the former verdict. This person was not so wise as one Dinnis, who, having been condemned to die, escaped out of the liberty on the day fixed for his execution (which might be done by running in one direction about five hundred yards), and never returned. Meeting several people that asked if Dinnis was not to be beheaded on that day, his answer was, " I trow not," which, having some humour in it, became a proverbial saying in the district, and is used to this day—" 'I trow not,' quoth Dinnis." In the next place, the fact was to be proved in the clearest manner. The offender had to be taken either hand-habend or back-berand, that is, having the stolen goods in his hand, or bearing them on his back, or, lastly, confessing that he took them.

The value of the goods stolen had to be worth at least thirteenpence-halfpenny, or more. Taylor, the water-poet, refers to the subject as follows:

" At Halifax the law so sharpe doth deale,
　That whoso more than thirteenpence doth steale,
　They have a jyn that wondrous quick and well
　Sends thieves all headless into heaven or hell."

A further condition of the Halifax gibbet law is scarcely so clear as the preceding. The accused was, after three market or meeting days, within the town of Halifax, next after his apprehension and being condemned, taken to the gibbet. This probably means that after he was delivered to the bailiff, no time further than was necessary was to elapse before proceeding to the trial, and that the bailiff was to send speedy summons to those who were to try him, which might be done in two or three days. If he were found guilty, the day of his execution depended upon that of his sentence, for he was to be beheaded on no other day than Saturday, which was the great meeting. Thus, if condemned on Monday, he would be kept three market days; but if condemned on Saturday, as some assert, he would be conducted straightway to the gibbet. The two last persons who suffered death by this engine were condemned and executed on the same day.

The final ordinance of the law directs that on being led to the gibbet the malefactor is to have his head cut off from his body. That the machine was fully capable of this is evident both from Holinshed's remarks and from the following anecdote given by Wright, the historian of Halifax, as an extract from "A Tour through the Whole Island of Great Britain." A country woman, who was riding by the gibbet at the time of the execution of a criminal, had hampers at her sides, and the head, bounding to a considerable distance from the force of the descending axe, "jumped into one of the hampers, or, as others say, seized her apron with its teeth, and there stuck for some time."

The parish register at Halifax contains a list of forty-nine persons who suffered by the gibbet, commencing on the 20th day of March, 1541, the earliest date of which there is a recorded execution, and terminating on the 30th day of April, 1650, after which last execution the bailiff of the town received an intimation that should another case occur, he would be called to public account. The number of beheadals in each of the reigns comprised in the above dates are : five in the last six years of the reign of Henry VIII. ; twenty-five in the reign of Elizabeth ; seven in the reign of James I. ; ten in the reign of Charles I. ; two during the Commonwealth.

In the year 1650, John Hoyle made a drawing of the Halifax gibbet, which is regarded as a faithful representation of it. On the crown of the hill will be noticed a sketch of the ancient beacon.

An account of the last occasion upon which the services of the Halifax gibbet were called into requisition is interesting ; it is contained in a rare book. " Halifax and its Gibbet Law placed in a True Light." It was written by Dr. Samuel

Midgley, during an imprisonment for debt, and was published in 1708. " About the latter end of April, A.D. 1650, Abraham Wilkinson, John Wilkinson, and Anthony Mitchel were apprehended within the Manor of Wakefield and the liberties of Halifax, for divers felonious practices,

HALIFAX GIBBET, BY HOYLE.

and brought or caused to be brought into the custody of the chief bailiff of Halifax, in order to have their trials for acquittal or condemnation, according to the custom of the Forest of Hardwick, at the complaint and prosecution of Samuel Colbeck of Wardley, within the liberty of Halifax ; John Fielden of Stansfield, within the

said liberty ; and John Cusforth of Durker, in
the parish of Sandall, within the Manor of Wakefield." The Bailiff, according to the ancient
custom, issued a summons to the "several constables of Halifax, Sowerby, Warley, and Skir-
coat," charging them to appear at his house on
the 27th day of April, 1650, each accompanied by
four men, "the most ancient, intelligent, and of
the best ability" within his constabulary, to
determine the cases. The constables were
merely the law officers, the jurors being the
sixteen "most ancient men," and whose names
are given at length. They were empannelled in
a convenient room at the Bailiff's house, where
the accused and their prosecutors were brought
"face to face" before them, as also the stolen
goods, to be by them viewed, examined, and
appraised. The court was opened by the following address from the Bailiff: "Neighbours and
friends,—You are summoned hither and empannelled according to the ancient custom of the
Forest of Hardwick, and by virtue you are
required to make diligent search and inquiry
into such complaints as are brought against the
felons, concerning the goods that are set before
you, and to make such just, equitable, and faith-

ful determination betwixt party and party, as
you will answer between God and your own
conscience." He then addressed them on the
separate charges against the prisoners. From
Samuel Colbeck, of Warley, they were alleged to
have stolen sixteen yards of russet-coloured
kersey, which the jury valued at 1s. per yard.
Two of the prisoners were alleged to have stolen
from Durker Green, two colts, which were
produced in court, one of which was appraised at
£3, and the other at 48s. Also, Abraham
Wilkinson was charged by John Fielden with
stealing six yards of cinnamon-coloured kersey,
and eight yards of white " frized, for blankets."
After some debate concerning certain evidence
against the above, and " after some mature consideration, the jury, as is customary in such
cases," adjourned to the 30th day of April.
Upon this day they met, and after further full
examination gave their verdict in writing, and
directed that the prisoners Abraham Wilkinson
and Anthony Mitchel, " by ancient custom, and
liberty of Halifax, whereof the memory of man is
not to the contrary, the said Abraham Wilkinson
and Anthony Mitchel are to suffer death by
having their heads severed and cut off from their

bodies at the Halifax gibbet, unto which verdict we subscribe our names." The felons were executed upon the same day.

The stone scaffold or pedestal upon which the gibbet was erected was discovered by the Town Trustees in 1840, in attempting to reduce what was known as Gibbet Hill to the level of the neighbouring ground; and except some decay of the top and one of the steps, it is in a perfect state. It is carefully fenced round, and an inscription affixed, which was done at the cost of Samuel Waterhouse, Mayor, in 1852. The gibbet axe, formerly in the possession of the Lord of the Manor of Wakefield, is now preserved at the Rolls Office of that town. It weighs seven pounds twelve ounces; its length is ten inches and a half; it is seven inches broad at the top, and nearly nine at the bottom, and at the centre about seven and a half.

The Scottish Maiden.

Towards the middle of the sixteenth century the Earl of Morton, Regent of Scotland, during a visit to England, witnessed an execution at the Halifax gibbet. He appears to have been impressed in a favourable manner with the ingenuity of the machine, and gave directions for a model of it to be made. On his return home, in the year 1565, he had an instrument similar to the Halifax gibbet constructed. On account of remaining so long before it was used, so runs the popular story, it was known as " The Maiden." Rogers says that its appellation is from the Celtic *mod-dun*, originally signifying the place where justice was administrated. There is a popular notion that the first victim beheaded at the Maiden was the Earl of Morton. Such, however, was not the case, for he did not suffer death at it until June 2nd, 1581. " After ruling Scotland under favour of Elizabeth for nearly ten years," says a contributor to Chambers's " Book of Days," " Morton fell a victim to court faction, which probably could not have availed against him if he had not forfeited public esteem by his greed and cruelty. It must have been a striking sight when the proud, stern, resolute face, which had frowned so many better men down, came to speak from the scaffold, protesting his innocence of the crime for which he had been condemned, but owning sins enough to justify God for his fate." He died by the side of the City Cross, in High Street, Edinburgh, and for the next twelve months his head garnished a pinnacle on the neighbouring Tolbooth. It is generally agreed that the first time the Maiden was used was in the execution of the inferior agents in the assassination of Rizzio, which occurred at Holyrood Palace, on the 9th March, 1566. Some of

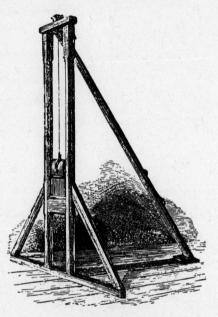

THE SCOTTISH MAIDEN.

the noblest men of Scotland suffered death by this instrument, and the long list of at least one hundred and twenty names includes those of Sir John Gordon of Haddo; President Spottiswoode; the Marquis and Earl of Argyle. The latter nobleman, "when stepping on the scaffold," says Daniel Wilson, "and preparing to lay his head on the block, is reported to have said, with grave humour worthy of Sir Thomas More: ' It was the sweetest maiden he had ever kissed.' "

In the year 1710, the use of the maiden was discontinued. It may now be seen in the Museum of the Society of Antiquaries of Scotland, at Edinburgh.

THE END

Index.